Dead Ground

•

Dead Ground, Live Ground, Dead Ground:
a soldier from 3 Scots, The Blackwatch, searching for IEDs.

Dead Ground
2018–1918

•

Edited by

Andrew McNeillie and
James McNeillie

First published in 2018 by Clutag Press
PO BOX 154, Thame, OX9 3RQ

A CIP record for this title is available from the British Library.

ISBN 978–1–9997178–6–5

Printed and bound in Great Britain by TJ International Ltd, Padstow, Cornwall

Contents

Notes on Contributors

Mark Adams is a former Royal Marine.

Patrick Bishop is a noted author on military subjects and a war correspondent, working for many years on the *Daily Telegraph*. His books include the immensely influential *3 PARA. Afghanistan, Summer 2006 THIS is War* (2007) and (with Eamon Mallie) *The Provisional IRA* (1987).

John Brannigan lives in Belfast and teaches English at University College Dublin. His most recent book is *Archipelagic Modernism: Literature in the Irish and British Isles, 1890–1970* (2015).

Gordon Campbell is a traveller, scholar and former Foreign Office adviser. His most recent journey was to Greenland, where the edges of the retreating dead ice are teaming with life. He is also a noted linguist, an authority on the Renaissance period and a biographer and editor of John Milton.

Tony Crowley is Professor of English at Leeds. Born and raised in Liverpool, he has published widely on the politics of language and the murals of Northern Ireland. His latest publications include *The Liverpool English Dictionary* (2017) and the online archive: 'The murals of Northern Ireland 1979–2017'.

Damian Walford Davies is Head of the School of English, Communication and Philosophy at Cardiff University. His most recent books include, as editor, *Roald Dahl: Wales of the Unexpected* (2016) and the poetry collections *Judas* (2015) and *Alabaster Girls* (2015). Forthcoming are the co-edited volume *Romantic Cartographies* and the edited collection *Counterfactual Romanticism*.

Douglas Dunn is the author of more than ten collections of poetry, including his latest *The Noise of a Fly* (2017). He was awarded the Queen's Medal for Poetry in 2013. Until recently he was a Professor of English at the University of St Andrews.

Peter Gill has been a foreign correspondent for most of a career and has covered his fair share of wars. His first was the Indo-Pakistan war of 1971 for the *Daily Telegraph* which led him on East to the American war in Vietnam. He was one of the few correspondents to stay behind in Saigon after the Fall. For ITV current affairs he made a series of films in Afghanistan during the Soviet occupation of the 1980s. He went back recently to research a book on aid workers and the 'war on terror', his fifth book on the aid industry.

Vesna Goldsworthy is Professor of Creative Writing at the Universities of Exeter and East Anglia. She has authored five internationally best-selling and award winning books, two of which—a memoir, *Chernobyl Strawberries*, and a novel, *Gorsky*—have been serialised by the BBC.

John Greening's recent books include a memoir of two years in Egypt, *Threading a Dream*, an edition of Geoffrey Grigson's poetry, and his own collection, *To the War Poets*. He edited the OUP edition of Edmund Blunden's *Undertones of War*.

Paul Hodgson was born in Shrewsbury in 1972. A graduate of the Royal College of Art, he is a visual artist who creates hybrid works that incorporate paint, digital print and photography. Solo exhibitions include Marlborough Fine Art, London; University of Cambridge; and Feigen Contemporary, New York.

Andrew Kahn teaches Russian literature at Oxford. He has written about the politicisation of Mandelstam's Anglo-American reputation in the West during the Cold War and, with Kenneth Haynes, a study of Geoffrey Hill's engagement with Mandelstam's poetry. He has published a book about Alexander Pushkin and is co-author of the *Oxford History of Russian Literature* (2018).

Tim Kendall is Professor of English at the University of Exeter. Author of several books on modern poets, he has also edited an anthology of First World War verse for OUP and *The Norton Anthology of Poetry*. He is presenter of a documentary on Ivor Gurney, and Producer of a documentary on Sylvia Plath (both BBC).

James Macdonald Lockhart's first book, *Raptor: A Journey Through Birds* was published in 2016. He lives near Oxford.

Don McCullin is a photojournalist of world renown, celebrated for his courage and compassion, in covering both war and social hardship, producing images of iconic status. He was knighted in 2017.

Patrick McIlroy is a former Royal Marine.

Kate McLoughlin is a Professor of English Literature at the University of Oxford. She is the author of *Veteran Poetics: British Literature in the Age of Mass Warfare* (2018), *Authoring War: The Literary Representation of War from the Iliad to Iraq* (2011) and *Martha Gellhorn: The War Writer in the Field and in the Text* (2007). In 2009, she edited *The Cambridge Companion to War Writing*.

Andrew McNeillie is a publisher and runs the Clutag Press which also publishes the literary magazine *Archipelago* under his editorship. His most recent book of poems *Making Ends Meet* was published in 2017. He is an Emeritus Professor of Exeter University.

James McNeillie is a lawyer.

Leo Mellor is the Roma Gill Fellow in English at Murray Edwards College, University of Cambridge. His first book was *Reading the Ruins: Bombsites, Modernism and British Culture* (2011) and he also recently edited a special issue of *Critical Quarterly* on 'the long 1930s'.

Andrew Motion is the co-founder of the Poetry Archive and was UK Poet Laureate from 1995 to 2009. He is now Homewood Professor of the Arts at Johns Hopkins University and lives in Baltimore.

Jeremy Mynott is the author of *Birdscapes: birds in our imagination and experience* (2009), *Thucydides* (2013), *Knowing your Place* (2016), and most recently *Birds in the Ancient World: winged words* (2018). He is a founder member of 'New Networks for Nature'.

Seamus Perry is a Fellow of Balliol College, Oxford, where he is Tutor in English Literature. He is, with Christopher Ricks and Freya Johnston, editor of the journal *Essays in Criticism*.

Nicholas Pierpan is a playwright, screenwriter, and poet. He is a lecturer in Creative Writing at Royal Holloway, University of London, and the Creative Arts Fellow at Wolfson College, Oxford.

Sean Power is a former soldier and photographer.

Alan Riach is Professor of Scottish Literature at Glasgow University, general editor of Hugh MacDiarmid's collected works, and author of numerous articles and books, including co-editorship of *The Edinburgh Companion to Twentieth-Century Scottish Literature* (2009) and *Scotlands: Poets and the Nation* (2004). Like MacDiarmid, he has published acclaimed English-language versions of the great Gaelic poems of the eighteenth century: Duncan Ban MacIntyre's *In Praise of Ben Dorain* (2014) and Alasdair Mac Mhaighster Alasdair's *The Birlinn of Clanranald* (2015). His most recent collection of poems *The Winter Book* appeared in 2017.

Christopher Ricks, a Professor of Humanities at Boston University, was Professor of Poetry at Oxford University 2004–9. Widely acknowledged to be our greatest living literary critic, he is also an editor, notably of Tennyson and T. S. Eliot, and currently of the writings of the Victorian lawyer, judge and essayist James Fitzjames Stephen. He is the author of a pioneering major study (2004) of the songs of 2016's Nobel Laureate for Literature Bob Dylan. Christopher served in the British Army, with the Green Howards, in Egypt 1953–4.

Ian Ritchie is a Royal Academician and elected member of the Akademie der Künste. He leads one of the world's most original and influential architectural practices. He is Visiting Professor of Architecture Liverpool University and has chaired many international juries including the RIBA Stirling Prize. Ian has written several books, including poetry, and his art is held in several international galleries and museums.

Fiona Stafford is Professor of English at Somerville College, Oxford, where she works on Romantic literature, Scottish and Irish poetry, Literature and the Visual Arts, Nature Writing, new and old. Recent books include *Local Attachments* (2010), *Reading Romantic Poetry* (2012), *The Long, Long Life of Trees* (2016), *Jane Austen: A Brief Life* (2017). She is currently writing the Romantic Period volume of The Oxford History of English Literature and a brief book about flowers.

Peter Stothard is a classicist and the author of four books of memoir, most recently *The Senecans: Four Men and Margaret Thatcher*. He is a former editor of *The Times* and the *TLS*. 'Henry versus Herbert' is from work in progress on *Romans and Britons: From the Beatles' first LP to Brexit*.

Alice Spawls is an editor at the *London Review of Books*. She writes about art and other things for the *LRB*, the *NYRB*, the *Guardian*, *FT*, *TLS* (where a version of this essay first appeared) and *Apollo*. She is a cofounder of Silver Press, which publishes neglected or under-esteemed writing by women.

Brian Turner is an American poet and essayist. He served in the US Army in Iraq and in Bosnia and Herzegovina. His award-winning debut collection of poems *Here, Bullet* (2005) was followed by *Phantom Noise* (2010), a book shortlisted for the T. S. Eliot Prize. *My Life as a Foreign Country: A Memoir* was published in 2014. He is Director of a Master of Fine Arts program at Sierra Nevada College at Lake Tahoe.

Introduction

'DEAD GROUND' in military terms is terrain into which you cannot see. What is visible there may deceive you by concealment. If you are within it, on the other hand, believing you're invisibly hidden, you may be mistaken. You can never quite be sure you're not observed or otherwise detected from some vantage point or other. We use the term here as a kind of metaphor, in a wide-ranging way. In our view war is itself a dead ground, where victory and defeat are concealed from view, where policy, stratagem, and brutality manoeuvre in the mind, and unforeseen consequences and desperate measures run wild in the world. It sounds simplistic but bears saying (again and again): in war people are killed or maimed, soldier and civilian alike, in terrible circumstances, the old and the young—'wounded children marooned in their pain' as Brian Turner puts it. There is 'collateral' everywhere, which is to say, euphemism. It's a story as old as time and one without end. One in which ultimately the soldiers fight and die not for Queen and Country or the State but for each other.

From which we conclude, that perhaps the most significant stretch of dead ground is that between our ears. We do not know what our minds conceal from us, as to motive, and justification. Though we might persuade ourselves we do, adequately at least, to see green for go in place of red for danger, when the group-think fever takes us, the patriotic mist descends on parliament. We may be accountable but we are not quite responsible. That is the human factor at work. That is the human condition. The cause is declared just. Terms and conditions are agreed that will soon enough be blown away. ('Mission creep' will set in.) Action must be taken, now or never. Shock-and-awe! here we go. Politicians and press are now gung-ho, as they say, and sure it will all be over by Christmas. So it was in 1914. Is there anything more to be said? There is, a lot more—how long have you got?—and some of it is said in this book.

*   *   *

The First World War was a seismic convulsion in the plate-tectonics of empire of an unprecedented order. If there were a Richter Scale of War, then the First World War would measure 10, the all-time high at that point in European and world history. As is by now commonplace to acknowledge, its shocks and aftershocks went on being registered down the two decades to the next quake, one of even greater, global magnitude, requiring us to recalibrate Richter.

Far from being 'The War That Will End War' as H. G. Wells in 1914 declared or willed it to be, it was a conflict that would trigger others. It helped enable revolutionary upheavals right from its epicentre—1916, in Ireland; 1917 in Russia—events that still rumble on, in the 21st century, even after the Good Friday Agreement of 1998/9 or the breaching of the Berlin Wall in 1989 and the subsequent collapse of the Soviet Union.

The combined death toll of the First World War and its aftermath is effectively incalculable. But as it ground on, bogged down in, as we say, Flanders Fields, an entire generation of young German, French and British men was decimated on a scale never witnessed before, by means never seen before, in the form of tank, aerial and otherwise mechanised warfare. And there were other fronts as well, along the Austro-Hungarian and the Ottoman fault-lines, with their own tragically high casualty counts; and out on the high seas, where terrible calamities occurred.

Most ominously the First World War inaugurated the random bombing (and shelling, as at Scarborough) of civilian targets and so heralded a future form of 'total war'. The trialling of the Luftwaffe in the Spanish Civil War, the London blitz, the flattening of Coventry, and the carpet-bombing of Dresden would follow in due course. All to be taken to another apocalyptic level in Japan with the use of the Atomic Bomb. The Holocaust was of course quite another matter, a moral dead ground and in physical terms 'invisible' until Allied forces stumbled on Belsen, Auschwitz, Dachau and the rest. It is not part of the story here. Which is emphatically not to suggest the scale and nature of its horror is lost on anyone in these pages.

Everywhere we look in the wake of the First World War we see generally disastrous consequences. This was of course most dramatically the case within Europe itself. The punitive reparations imposed by the Treaty of Versailles of 1919 contributed directly to the imminent economic implosion of Germany and helped fuel the rise of Nazism. It is by now a well-worn story but even as the Treaty was being drafted some—most notably the economist J. M. Keynes who was party to the negotiations—foresaw what its economic consequences would be. The only true positive to the war was that it shook the British class system to its foundations, and so helped enable concessions that improved franchise.

Beyond Europe, the conflict provided Britain and France (and temporarily Russia's Tsarist regime) with imperialist opportunity. Nowhere was this more tellingly so than in the Arab World. The Sykes-Picot Asia-Minor Agreement, secretly reached in 1916, would lead to the League of Nations-endorsed Anglo-Iraqi Treaty of 1922, whereby Iraq was created, as a British Mandate under Sunni leadership, arbitrarily within lines for the most part drawn on the map of Mesopotamia. Sykes-Picot is reviled by the descendants of those on whom it was first imposed, as was made more than plain in 2016 at its centenary, and with good reason. When Tony Blair insists, on the surface not unreasonably, that the world is a better place without Saddam Hussein, he neglects to say for *whom* and *when*. He cannot see or afford to admit that his late imperialism is Sykes-Picot by other means, with more immediately disastrous consequences.

The consequences of such divisions of the spoils as that agreement enabled are ones with which people in the West are presently far more aware than perhaps ever before. As for Sykes-Picot, so for the Balfour

Declaration of 1917 in support of a national home in Palestine for the Jewish people. These measures made in 'good faith', but made blindly, with great arrogance, took little or no account of the realities on the ground. They showed no respect for indigenous peoples, their cultures, faiths and existing tribal and territorial alignments. Whatever the rights and wrongs, they sowed, and restlessly helped germinate, the seeds of seemingly endless conflict between irreconcilable parties and factions. The editors here take no sides on this matter. They merely state historical fact.

It's a truism that where politics is concerned, hindsight is not 20:20, or we'd have no need to write history. Cause and effect, insofar as they might be identified, whether in parliaments or on the battlefield, are better examined in terms of chaos theory and the nature of unintended consequences than the supposed light of reason. There is certainly no monopoly on wisdom. But still some choices are wiser than others, even in the here and now, as everyone knows in daily life. Wise choices are made all the time. But it was unwise, for example, to allow the assassination in Sarajevo of Archduke Franz Ferdinand any part in influencing a decision to go to war. Wisdom then went out of the window.

The origins of that war dated back to the Prussian victory over France in 1870. Stresses had been mounting ever since. The continental plates of imperial rivalry were grinding away under the political crust and not that far from the surface either. In the absence of intelligent conversation between the Powers, it was only a matter of time before the ground shook and shook so hard that Europe tottered into chaos and slaughter. In very many, perhaps in most respects the First World War ought to have been an avoidable one. Lest we forget: it wasn't. The remembrance culture, honouring the dead—'At the going down of the sun and in the morning'—reminds us of that every year. But still we go to war even when unexplored alternatives stare us in the face.

You can make your own list of similarly unwise moments and ill-considered capitulations into war. There are enough of them. At its top might be the West's more recent regime-change/nation-building adventures. But nothing will unmake such decisions, nothing will predict them for the future, and nothing will prevent their like being made again and again, try as hard as we might. Human beings are first and foremost fallible and they are tribal. It was the tribal element in the ritual at the Cenotaph that so vexed the poet Philip Larkin.

It is not this book's intention to claim high ground, or indeed all the dead ground, in terms of major conflicts since 1918. This is not an academic study planned to cover all the bases. It is a gathering of literary writing and reportage with some photographs and artwork, images of war-art, from the trenches to the murals of the north of Ireland. Nor do we set out to call for a world in which there are no more wars. Tyrants, megalomaniacs, ideologues—fanatics of all kinds—are hardly going to listen or have a change of heart. They will, and do, chance their arm if they can. That is the nature of the beast.

It is depressing but realistic to accept that in certain circumstances not to act militarily can also be a mistake. Not to have gone to war against Hitler and the Nazis would have proved an unspeakable disaster. Not to have sought to decapitate DAESH, as far as it is possible to decapitate a hydra, would also have been disastrous. But a 'necessary' war is a rare thing, as rare almost as a bee in snow. Now innumerable wars—'proxy' wars, civil strife in failed States—and talk of wars in the form of 24/7 TV coverage tend to inure us to what war really means. And don't let us forget war's illegitimate offspring, famine, either, as Peter Gill forcibly reminds us.

What is it they say of terrorists? They have only to succeed once. Their enemies have to succeed all the time. We only have to leap once, say in the spirit of Rupert Brooke's 'swimmers into cleanness leaping'— from, ironically, his 1914 poem 'Peace'—to make the biggest mistake of our lives and, more to the point, the lives of others, of 'the other'. Just as it's a long way to Tipperary from the Somme, it's a long way back from anywhere once war is declared and no strategy ever holds its ground all the way to what passes for victory. It's a long way back from Afghanistan for sure, where the lessons of history fall forever on deaf ears in the lunatic pursuit of what Kipling famously called 'The Great Game'. To err is human, we all know. Two err twice is regrettable but to keep on erring, to 'Carry on Up the Khyber' as they say in Ealing, and to do so time and time again, to disastrous result, surely suggests some people need their heads examining. What goes on in the dead ground there?

* * *

The First World War gave unprecedented rise not only to mechanical warfare, but to quite another, ultimately life-enhancing phenomenon: a new literature (and new forms of art)—a poetry of protest, suffering, and pity; with accompanying memoir—written by men, officers and men, who fought and in some cases perished in battle. Many of these are household names in many households. Among the readers of this book, who will not have heard of Wilfred Owen, Siegfried Sassoon, Edward Thomas, Robert Graves, Edmund Blunden, Ivor Gurney, Isaac Rosenberg, David Jones, or deluded Rupert Brooke? Of course the list of soldier poets is far longer than that, as is the life of what is known as 'war poetry', poetry written by non-combatants.

It is from a poem by a non-combatant that this book takes its title. Henry Reed was born in the year the First Word War began its tragic funeral march to Armistice Day. He became a journalist and went on to work at the Foreign Office (1942–5), after which he turned his hand again to writing, most notably for the BBC. His single book of poems *A Map of Verona* was published in 1946. It included 'Lessons of the War', a triptych of great technical accomplishment and feeling. 'Judging Distances', the second of these poems, is reprinted in full as an extended epigraph to this book.

In 'Judging Distances' we overhear an NCO instructing new recruits how to go about reading a map, maps being '… of time, not place, so far as the army/Happens to be concerned'—against which the poet in a kind of running commentary assumes another voice, expanding on and undercutting the lesson, to gently satirical and poignantly lyrical effect. The instructor finally warns against the possibility of there being 'dead ground in between', ground that might conceal an enemy or other hazard, between where we are and where we need to get to. It is an ancient military preoccupation. Julius Caesar was particularly obsessed by it. Radar operators too would later have their own version of it, as has been reflected on elsewhere by Peter Stothard. Dead ground as terrain is very much a matter of angles. 'Dead angle' is the closest the term comes to the Oxford English Dictionary, as Christopher Ricks reveals to us, and even then it is fittingly almost hidden from view.

As said at the outset, in making this book we have taken the idea of 'dead ground' as a far-ranging metaphor, providing a variety of angles at which to consider war and the consequences of war, its pervasiveness: its human cost, in terms of body count and mental health, and what happens in its aftermath, by way of famine and disease, and further wars. We look too at war's capacity to allow new tyrannies to emerge, even as it opposes tyranny, as is most notably to be found in the creation and dissolution of the Soviet Union but also more pressingly than ever, perhaps, in the Arab world of today.

We also explore war's impact on domestic life; and on Nature, on land and landscape, both on the battlefield and the home front, on MoD firing ranges, at listening posts—in what Leo Mellor calls 'Forbidden Landscapes' and James Macdonald Lockhart in his example terms 'Live Ground'.

But all is not doom and gloom and abrasion. This is also very much a book about landscape and place, about the human spirit, about Nature's resilience, even, paradoxically perhaps about a species of hope in fortitude. Time and again in the pages here we are reminded of the aesthetics of place, visually, acoustically, and temporally.

Soldiers are students of landscape and so must those be who write about war from the frontline. Hyper-vigilance does not make them immune to beauty. On the contrary, it heightens awareness of the physical world, of nature and weather, skylines, sunset and sunrise, and night, clear nights when the galaxies loom largest. Immersed in the elemental, living rough, as we might say, out in the field in all weathers, training there and fighting, they are feral. They come closer to primitive experience than civilians might, this side of the war zone, even on the most adventurous of adventure holidays. To dwell in extremis is to *be*, to live in the moment, and by doing so to know something intense about life, about mortality, something spiritually meaningful. Most soldiers know what it is like to hallucinate from being pushed to their physical limits. Such experiences can intoxicate, are indeed a form of intoxication. They too are a feature of warfare.

But as we know it can all topple in an instant into living hell, as notably it did in Flanders, day in day out, year in year out. The war artist Paul Nash, like Wilfred Owen on the subject of poetry and pity, having experienced shell barrages and poison gas attacks, soon saw himself as 'no longer an artist', as Alice Spawls tells us. Now for Nash sunrise and sunset were 'blasphemous … mockeries to man'. There were no highs, no heightened moments of reflection.

Then coming out of battle can itself be catastrophic too. For many the horror of war begins when the battle or the war is over, when the mind breaks at last, under the after-shocks and flashbacks that now assail its delicate mechanisms.

* * *

The hard truth is that warfare is never stood down; it is always being waged, on one scale or another, somewhere, openly or covertly. It is the invisible map and infrastructure of what we call peace. It permeates the State just as it occupies portions of a nation's physical landscape.

Needs must as the devil drives … If you want a recommendation for further reading, we suggest Jonathan Swift's *Gulliver's Travels* (1726), for its scathing and sobering, historical witness to our perennial, incorrigible, proclivity for making war. But before you turn to Swift, we are sure you'll find much of great value to reflect on in this anthology of reportage, recollection, poems, essays and images, exploring its subject primarily, though not exclusively, from a British, and also an Irish, perspective. It is a relatively small patch of dead ground. None the less we hope it will make a fresh and stimulating intervention into the coming solemnities and the commercially opportunistic 'heritage' and 'legacy' contributions that will inevitably swarm into bookshop windows and onto shelves, onto television and cinema screens, on or around 11 November 2018, as the final centenary of 'The War That Will End War' is marked.

Some of our contributors are former soldiers. (One of them describes himself as a 'bootneck' as opposed to 'beatnik' poet.) Others are or have been eminent war correspondents, Foreign Office representatives, warzone photographers; one uses photography to create an ahistorical war-art; another is a major architect. Along with these are established poets, and brilliant critics. The contents have been ordered in what is broadly a reversed chronological order, as if from Armistice day 2018, to Armistice day 1918—or from Afghanistan to Flanders, a story in which the poppy so cherished as a symbol of remembrance in the one case figures also in a rather different light in the other, as itself a cause of wars.

Once the costs of production and publication of this book are met, all proceeds from its sale will go to appropriate charities.

Andrew McNeillie
James McNeillie

Judging Distances

Not only how far away, but the way you say it
Is very important. Perhaps you may never get
The knack of judging a distance, but at least you know
How to report on a landscape: the central sector,
The right of arc and that, which we had last Tuesday,
        And at least you know

That maps are of time, not place, so far as the army
Happens to be concerned—the reason being,
Is one which need not delay us. Again, you know
There are three kinds of tree, three only, the fir and the poplar,
And those which have bushy tops to; and lastly
        That things only seem to be things.

A barn is not called a barn, to put it more plainly,
Or a field in the distance, where sheep may be safely grazing.
You must never be over-sure. You must say, when reporting:
At five o'clock in the central sector is a dozen
Of what appear to be animals; whatever you do,
        Don't call the bleeders *sheep*.

I am sure that's quite clear; and suppose, for the sake of example,
The one at the end, asleep, endeavours to tell us
What he sees over there to the west, and how far away,
After first having come to attention. There to the west,
On the fields of summer the sun and the shadows bestow
        Vestments of purple and gold.

The still white dwellings are like a mirage in the heat,
And under the swaying elms a man and a woman
Lie gently together. Which is, perhaps, only to say
That there is a row of houses to the left of arc,
And that under some poplars a pair of what appear to be humans
    Appear to be loving.

Well that, for an answer, is what we might rightly call
Moderately satisfactory only, the reason being,
Is that two things have been omitted, and those are important.
The human beings, now: in what direction are they,
And how far away, would you say? And do not forget
    There may be dead ground in between.

There may be dead ground in between; and I may not have got
The knack of judging a distance; I will only venture
A guess that perhaps between me and the apparent lovers,
(Who, incidentally, appear now to have finished,)
At seven o'clock from the houses, is roughly a distance
    Of about one year and a half.

from Lessons of the War *by* HENRY REED

Dead Ground

•

Douglas Dunn

Dairsie War Memorial

Was it your wish—or is it our wish—
That you who died so very far away
Died to perpetuate your placid parish
Or the memory of a sunny harvest day?

Patrick Bishop

The Turbine

LOOKING DOWN the Sangin valley from the OP on the ridge just south of the Kajaki dam, Helmand looked gorgeous. Up here, the thumping heat of the plain was blunted by the breeze. The water pinned back by the dam walls sparkled in the sun and the fields spreading either side of the river were lush with crops. In between the maize rows men, women and kids were busy digging, pruning and carting stuff away. The bright blue burkas of the women and girls stood out from the grey-green foliage like patches of wild flowers.

'Bucolic,' I said. The word just came out.

'What?' The sergeant lowered his binoculars and glanced over.

'Nothing.' He went back to scouring the landscape. Jock's skin was scorched and flaking and his lips were chapped raw from days in the sun.

Sound carried weirdly from below. You could hear a moped crawling along the 611 highway even though it was three or four miles away. The buzz just emphasised the stillness.

We all knew it would not last much longer. Down below a Para patrol was moving south down the highway—a grandiose name for a ten-metre wide band of stony track. They were heading for a couple of insurgent positions a mile or so ahead—'Sentry Compound' and 'Big Top'. The patrol had not advanced far when there was a crackle of light arms fire from the enemy lines. The response was immediate: a *thud-thud-thud*, followed by a swishing noise like waves lapping on a shore as the Paras' .50 calibre machine gun teams lying up in the high ground above the highway answered back.

The firing died away and the valley was quiet again. The workers in the fields had carried on throughout as if nothing was happening.

Then, down below at the foot of our hill there was a puff of white smoke followed by a flat bang. 'Mortar' said someone, and all binoculars swivelled to the west, over the barren strip of land dotted with abandoned baked-mud compounds on the far bank of the river. There was a flash and another harmless explosion a few hundred metres away. It was enough to leave a radar trace that gave away the firing point.

Soon there was a new sound: a sort of slithering as 105mm artillery shells spun overhead. Silently, white smoke pillars, stained with pulverised earth, started to rise from the barren fields.

It went on like this all morning. After each spate of banging, the silence flooded swiftly in to fill the spaces between the explosions. Eventually the peasants downed tools—not because of the shooting but because it was time to eat.

So much of the soldiers' work was like this. They stepped out of their makeshift forts each morning to trail their coats and goad the enemy into having a go. Sooner or later, they obliged. The insurgents attacked with World War Two vintage AK47 rifles and Rocket Propelled Grenades. The invaders then hammered them with the most sophisticated and expensive weaponry the defence industry could provide. The imbalance was blackly absurd. But for all invaders' advantages, they never seemed to prevail. No matter how many hi-tech bombs they rained down on the insurgents, once the smoke cleared, there they were again. Two years into the British arrival in Helmand, the whole thing was starting to look like a waste of money, time and lives.

This morning though, things felt different. For once it seemed that the violence might have some meaning. All this prodding and probing was to a purpose. By 'suppressing' the fighters in the valley, the Paras were preparing the ground for a different sort of operation, one that would add some substance to the claim that they were in Helmand not to fight but to help. There was a rare whiff of optimism in the kiln-hot air. All this effort was in aid of an Operation called Oqab Tsuka—Eagle's Summit in Pashto. It was the sort of project that the troops were supposed to have been engaged in but rarely were. Its success would at last inject some meaning into the soldiers' presence. It would be, as one of them said to me, 'something our parents will understand.'

Though it was hard to credit now, Western efforts to improve life in the area stretched back decades. Back in the early Nineteen Fifties, the Export-Import Bank of the United States (the credit export agency of the US government) funded the building of a dam and power house to bring electricity to the villages of the long fertile ribbon that stretches either side of the Helmand river. Originally three turbines were planned, providing enough surplus power to augment supplies to the city of Kandahar, about seventy miles as the crow flies to the south east. Afghanistan's miserable recent history of invasion and internecine war had prevented the installation of the third.

In 2004, while the area was relatively peaceful, the Americans carried out some much-needed repair work at the dam and their USAID development agency awarded a contract to a Chinese company to design and build a third turbine generator to boost capacity. When British troops deployed in the area in the spring of 2006, Kajaki became their responsibility. However, they were too busy trying to contain the uprising that had followed their arrival to do anything more than prevent the dam from falling into insurgent hands.

The early days of the British campaign had been a story of blunders followed by crises. What was originally intended as a reconstruction mission swiftly degenerated into a series of desperate actions fought in remote outposts, far beyond the boundaries of the original intended area of operations.

At the fighting core of the first deployment were two battalions of the Parachute Regiment. Their exploits, at the sieges of Sangin, Musa Qaleh and elsewhere were now embedded in regimental legend. As a result of my account of the episode in a bestselling book called *3 Para*, the British public knew all about them as well.

Since the 'break-in battle', as the events of the summer of 2006 had now been designated by the military (thus suggesting they had expected a big fight all along) the situation had stabilised to the point where attention could focus on doing something more than the endless pointless gavottes of provocation and retaliation. In the spring of 2008, a team of sixty British officers began planning for Oqab Tsuka. The goal was to deliver, after a thirty-three year delay, the third turbine to the Kajaki Dam. It was billed as a classic counter-insurgency effort. The people, so ran the mantra, were the prize. Installing the new machinery would bring light to the dark villages and boost the economy of Kandahar, Afghanistan's second city.

The operation coincided with the Paras return to theatre. Much had changed in two years, including many of the players. No-one hangs around in any one job or outfit for long in the modern army, especially if you are an officer. Colonel Stuart who led 3 Para into Helmand had been promoted out of the Paras. Colonel Huw, his former 2–i–C was now the boss. The two were chalk and cheese. Stuart was slight, intellectually restless, full of nervous energy. He spoke in a clipped accent and was in a hurry to get to the top. Huw was quiet, methodical, and his background was not that different to those he led. I'd seen them both up close and liked them; different sorts of soldiers but both good leaders in their different ways.

Many of the veterans of 2006 had moved on. They had been replaced by an influx of young men who had yet to see action. It was with mixed feelings that I learned that some of them had joined up after reading my book. There were plenty who did not mind admitting that they had volunteered in the hope of tasting just the sort of desperate close-quarters fighting described in *3 Para*.

Operation Oqab Tsuka looked as if it would give them all the action they were looking for. The job of 3 Para, along with 2 Para with whom they shared a sort of sibling rivalry and various other 'atts and dets' would be to provide the security for the convoy that was to deliver the machinery from Kandahar to Kajaki on the last, most vulnerable stage of the journey.

The turbine was nothing fancy, a Chinese-made type that had been tried and tested all over the world. It weighed 220 tonnes in total and its main component parts were too heavy to be lifted into place by the faithful Chinooks that hauled men and supplies all around the country. The C-130 transports in theatre could handle the loads, and there was an abandoned Soviet-built airstrip next to the dam that could have been patched up easily enough. The problem was getting the kit across the river. It was spanned by a scaffolding bridge that would collapse under the weight of a heavily-laden lorry. Building a new one was dismissed as too time-consuming and expensive. So the decision was taken that after the parts had been delivered to Kandahar Airfield they would go the rest of the way by road.

The initial plan had been to send the convoy westwards from Kandahar to Lashkar Gah along the metalled Highway 1, then north up the 611. It was here that the trouble was almost certain to begin. This was bandit country. On either side lay humid fields of high crops— the 'Green Zone'—which provided perfect cover for attacks. There was a further high risk from planted roadside bombs—IEDs—as well as 'legacy mines' left from the Soviet occupation. The insurgents would have plenty of warning of the convoy's arrival, and could mount their attacks at leisure as it lumbered along.

The planners had considered bribing their way through: enough dollars paid to the right tribal figures might result in them staying the hand of the insurgents. The idea was dropped on the grounds that the chances of anyone honouring the agreement were slight.

Then the Pathfinder Platoon, a dashing reconnaissance unit, had come up with an alternative route that greatly reduced the risks. While reconnoitring the area they stumbled on a well-used track that ran across the mountains flanking the river. It had been adopted by the inhabitants of the valley as a way of getting to Kandahar without taking the main road. A taxi driver explained its advantages to one of the Pathfinders. It meant, he explained 'that I don't get jerked around by the insurgents, I don't pay road tax to the Afghan National Police, I'm not robbed by the Afghan Army and there aren't any IEDs.' In a sentence he had summed up the miserable insecurity of peasant life in a lawless and callous world.

From the planners' point of view the route was a godsend. It ran across open ground with nowhere for the insurgents to hide. Not only was the surface hard enough to take heavily-loaded vehicles. It also made it easier to spot IEDs. Protecting the convoy was now much less daunting. It was only in the last few miles of the journey, when the vehicles would have to rejoin the 611 and the Green Zone south of the dam that things became more difficult. That was where the Paras came in.

It was the Royal Logistical Corps, though, that bore most of the responsibility for getting the turbine to Kajaki. The loggies were the biggest outfit in the British Army—the 'Really Large Corps' as they pointed out with defensive pride. But the unglamorous nature of their work meant that no-one outside the military had ever heard of them. Its members were used to being taken for granted. Now they would have their hour in the sun, and they were looking forward to it.

D-Day was set at 27 August. A five-kilometre long snake of heavy equipment transporters, supply lorries, tankers and armoured vehicles would set off in the dark and travel thirty kilometres west along the tarmacked road before turning north into the desert. From there to Kajaki was another seventy kilometres. How long it would take was anyone's guess but a sober estimate taking account of breakdowns, mine clearance etc, estimated it would proceed at about one kilometre an hour. Ultimately it depended on the Taliban.

As the commander of the operation, Brigadier Mark pointed out, this term was merely a label rather than a definition. It bundled together religious ideologues, criminals and opportunists, who for the time being at least had a shared interest in fighting the foreigners and the government.

Most of the men on the ground didn't spend much time analysing their motives. At first there had been some respect for the mad courage of the enemy. Now they were simply men who had killed and maimed their comrades and were out to kill and maim them. Their cause was incomprehensible. Afghanistan was a gigantic shithole. The Brits were here to clean it up but these guys were willing to fight to the death to keep it that way.

The Paras had a reputation for enjoying the 'kinetic' part of soldiering (to use the current euphemism) over the more constructive aspects of the soldiers' trade. But as they prepared to clear the way for the convoy in the Green Zone hideouts of the enemy, the tattooed Toms seemed just as excited as everyone else by the thought of a little nation building.

There was one quarter, however, where enthusiasm for the adventure was limited. Hugh, the Foreign Office representative in the area, did not bother disguising his deep scepticism. It was all very well getting the turbine there, he pointed out. But what happened next? How was the Alliance going to find the manpower to supervise the construction of the power lines to carry away the electricity? And who was going to guard them from insurgent sabotage?

Hugh's voice was drowned out by official applause for the project, amplified by the media who were keen to lighten the gloom that had settled over the Afghanistan story with a rare glimmer of good news.

In the early hours of the morning of 28 August, the convoy ground through the gates of KAF, carrying the seven components of the turbine, encased in armour plating, and the hopes of the international alliance in Afghanistan.

For weeks before, the Paras had been preparing the ground. Teams had been aggressively patrolling north of Sangin. The idea was to fool the insurgents into thinking the convoy was coming that way, while beating them up in the process and reducing their capacity to cause trouble when they learned the truth.

Five days before D-Day, 500 Paras arrived at the dam, along with a *kandak* of 400 men from the Afghan National Army (ANA) and began pushing down the 611 to secure the last leg of the convoy's journey.

From the Sparrowhawk OP we had a grandstand view. To civilian eyes the overmatch in weaponry and numbers seemed almost embarrassing. The occasional volleys and mortar rounds from the insurgents seemed to have been fired more for form than effect. It began to seem that the convoy might breeze in unmolested.

Then came news that there might be no shots fired at all. The Kajaki district leader Abdul Razzak suggested he might be able to arrange a ceasefire with the insurgent leaders. Abdul Razzak was built like a grizzly bear with thick black glossy hair and beard. His permanent smile did nothing to dispel an air of menace. Despite working for the government and allying with the invaders he managed to keep a foot in both camps. The insurgents had murdered his brother, but to occupy any position of authority in Afghanistan, you had to stay flexible if you wanted to stay alive.

In the last days of August, while the troops were securing the highway Abdul Razzak took British and Afghan officers to two shuras with local elders. They urged the elders to persuade the fighters to leave the convoy alone. Its safe arrival was in everyone's interests. In addition, the Brits offered 25,000 dollars for community projects for the 5,000 inhabitants of Kajaki Sofla, and a promise that once the convoy had passed through they would stay away.

The elders seemed friendly and well-disposed. There were many expressions of friendship and good intentions. They departed to pass on the message, returning after a few hours with some fantastic news. The insurgents not only agreed to a ceasefire. They were also willing to remove overnight IEDs planted along the route. After some toing and froing, it was agreed to meet the following morning to finalise the deal.

There was satisfaction in the Kajaki camp that night. Even the most ardent of the young Toms was sated with fighting. The insurgents had taken a hammering, losing according to a rough intelligence estimate, two hundred out of five hundred fighters killed or wounded. So far there had been no civilian casualties—though that could easily change if it came to close quarters combats in heavily-populated Kajaki Sofla.

We set off after breakfast to meet the elders, with Abdul Razzak in the lead vehicle. When we arrived at the rendezvous, a clump of trees by the roadside where plastic chairs and cheap carpets had been set out. The place was empty. As the minutes passed, the mood sagged. Then

Abdul Razzak made a call on his mobile satphone. He switched it off and shook his head. The elders would not be coming. The insurgents' leaders in Pakistan, it emerged later, had vetoed the deal.

For the rest of the day, the work of securing the route continued, occupying the compounds on either side of the 611. I spent it with Colonel Huw just behind the lead troops. Early on he asked for one of the fast jets patrolling high above to make a low pass, to let the insurgents know 'this is what we have and we are prepared to use it.' The plane came at 250 feet, shaking the mud walls of the compounds where the men in turbans and flip flops were waiting.

It made no difference. Soon afterwards the lead patrol was fired on from a compound. They paused and called in artillery and mortar fire. It arrived a few minutes later, landing with a crash and a flash, followed by silence. So it went on all day. Some insurgent positions proved particularly stubborn. Then the bombers were called in. I saw two GBU-38 satellite-guided bombs explode on a mud hut on a hillside, dropped by an aircraft that had flown in from Diego Garcia in the Indian Ocean. Each one cost a quarter of a million dollars, ten times what had been offered to the villagers.

By mid-afternoon the convoy had reached the highway and we drove down to meet it. All resistance had finished. On the way we passed a group of men and boys squatting under a tree in a dusty field. Around them, green flags flapped on tall poles. It was a graveyard and the men were there to bury someone. They looked at us with blank faces as our vehicle clattered past. When we returned, the group was still there. The ceremony was almost over and men were shovelling dirt onto the grave.

An interpreter went over to chat. He came back with the story. The mourners said the dead man was sitting on his moped when a rocket arrived from nowhere. 'They say he's just a farmer but I know he's a fucking Talib,' he said. In the background, another interpreter was repeating over and over again over a loudspeaker: 'Please leave this area because our soldiers are patrolling… stay in your compounds…. God be with you.'

It took the convoy seven hours to grind over the last eight kilometres of its journeys watched over by a line of sentries. Not a shot was fired at it. At 2am it arrived at Kajaki, looming out of the darkness in a cacophony of squealing, hissing brakes. The base troops came out with brews and cigarettes for the sleep-starved, knackered loggies. Everyone was smiling—grinning to each other with satisfaction, relief, and pride.

The following day we watched cranes start to unload the components off the transporters at a yard near the dam. There they stayed for many years. In the summer of 2011, a BBC journalist reported: 'The parts sit in broken packing cases or rusting freight containers, many of them exposed to the elements and overgrown with weeds.'

It appeared then that the scepticism of Hugh from the FCO had been justified and the soldiers' hopes of bringing progress self-deluding dreams. Op Oqab Tsuka seemed likely to be remembered only as a particularly rich example of the pointlessness of exerting yourself to do good in Afghanistan.

But British soldiers, strangely enough, believe in happy endings. If there is one quality they share it is a fundamental optimism, closely camouflaged though it may be by a cloak of cynicism. Nothing is usually quite as bad as it seems—and after a long wait, the story of the Kajaki Dam project seemed to show that they had been right all along about the value of Oqab Tsuka.

In August 2017 the USAID website reported that the turbine generator was finally up and running. It had been installed by the Afghan electricity and was rumbling away day and night adding 18.5 MW of power to the plant's output and 'delivering nearly double the amount of power to southern Afghanistan.'

Focusing—A soldier from the Royal Gurkha Rifles
preparing himself for a patrol in Nahr e Saraj.

Calm in the Storm: soldiers from A Coy, 3rd Battalion (the Black Watch) wait for
a storm to lift so a helicopter can come and collect them back to base.

Proving a Route or Walking the Line: a soldier from the 10 Queen's Own
Gurkha Logistics Regiment marks a clear route across a vulnerable
point for the armoured vehicles following him to cross.

Mark Adams

Recollections

I was nineteen-years-old when I joined the marines. I was on exercise in Cyprus when the planes hit the towers. We watched the flames and the dust and people running.

The following year we sailed out on warships and sat in the ocean off Iraq. We played cards and waited for the call and when it came we put all our personal possessions into storage and took our field kit and sat in the hold. Red lights and the hum of the plant machinery. Everyone sitting and sweating. Waiting for the helicopters.

When our turn came we stood on the loading lift. The sirens started shrieking and we came up out of the darkness into the first light of a balmy dawn. The navy ratings unclipped the chain and we marched off to load and make ready our weapons. We walked on to the helicopters in a practised order and sat in our places.

I wondered how it would get off the ground. There were bags all over and you had to struggle to do up the seatbelts because you had so much kit on. We heard the engines roar and we sank in our seats as the helicopter pulled clear of the deck. We felt the nose dip and our guts lurched as we swung down off the ship and started out across the water. Everyone was smiling.

We landed unopposed and sat there facing out into the desert. Sometimes a call would go up and we would put on our gas masks and lie there waiting with the eye glass misting over as we waited for the all clear. The day got hot as they lifted in all the wagons. We mounted up and swept off into the desert.

They said it would not rain and when it did we slept under the vehicles. The rain came hard. Big thick spots of it that would pockmark the earth and send up explosions of dust and sand. We would crawl under the wagons and rest on the dry sand. Mud stuck on our boots and in the end our bivvy bags were mired with filth and we would lie there together coiled like snakes. Sometimes if the rain kept on we would boil up water on our stoves and pass round a heavy metal mug of sweet tea that was hot enough to burn your hands.

I have the photographs of us dirty and white-toothed against our tans, smiling broadly in the mud with only the axle and the underside of the wagon visible overhead. Sandwiched between us and the under-side of the chassis was a black strip of rolling mud and sand below a thin strip of grey and stormy sky.

One day our position was between a bombed out building and a burning well. Our lungs would fill with black smoke or the smell of bodies rotting in the wreckage depending on the wind. I preferred the corpses. I figured it was less poisonous.

For a time it was mostly waiting. We would roll through positions and see nothing but abandoned field pieces and dirty weapons left heaped in huts and shellscrapes. Still warm stoves and scattered bags of rice. We were always moving. As we approached Basra we were laid up overnight in the desert and they fired the artillery line and we could see billows of flame lighting up the desert behind.

The deep concussive roars would roll out across the sand. There was the whistle of shells overhead in the darkness. Dull thumps of impact. In the morning when we walked out before the dawn, buildings were on fire. On the cars, the tires were still burning.

I could see the other men's faces lit up. They were darkscarred with dirt and camouflage cream and sallow like twisted jack-o-lanterns in the slow light of the coming dawn. Their eyes were hard, searching every hole and gap and street and window. It felt like the war of our dreams, of childhood movies long forgotten. We got shot at.

Your mind can't process what's going on and you laugh at the sheer outrageousness of it all. In a four hour gunfight everyone was wide-eyed and smiling. This was it. This was what we'd been waiting for our whole lives for. It was easy to enjoy it when you felt invincible.

You need to try and scoop bits of your friend's brain back into his skull before you can really speak with any weight on the matter. I did not do that. We had a few scratchy rushed contacts. We saw a lot more outgoing than incoming. Then it was over. It was not everything that I thought it would be.

*   *   *

Finishing up in Umm Qasr someone said it was like the diet coke of wars. I thought of all the Iraqi families that had lost loved ones. It probably felt more real to them. We left bodies in that place. We treated those we could, but sometimes they were just left with their blood spilling out onto the sand. Men were lost from the brigade but not from our unit. We watched RPGs bounce off wagons and fail to go off. We saw bullets go low and high and wide and ricochet humming into sand and scrub.

I will always feel like a slightly lesser man for that. There is always that reckless part of you that wants to know how you would have coped if things got really bad. When I talk to some people about the bad times they had on tours, I see them look away. I see them lost in some dark part of themselves as they repeat the details like they are reading from a script, without inflection or intonation. When I left the military I worked charity events for ex-forces. I saw some of the guys walking funny. Only afterward you found out they were a triple amputee. I saw some scars. Some I couldn't see.

You start to think of all those bedrooms preserved like dusty shrines by parents who don't know what to do with the hole that is left behind. Empty hallways and long drawn out days. Children learning about their fathers and mothers through photo albums. Many years from now they will wear the medals on the right side of their chest with an awful pride and try to honour a person they never got the chance to know.

And so it was enough. It was more than enough.

Still I will always feel a sliver of guilt that though I served, there were others that did much more. I think when people buy you a drink for your service they're not really buying it for you. They're buying it for the man that's not there. And when you drink, you drink to those left behind. You feel slightly embarrassed enjoying any privilege paid for with the lives of men that are no longer there to enjoy them.

You feel a certain weight of responsibility, to live the life they had taken from them. A friend from another unit was on a helicopter that went down. On a different day it could have been me. I remember some of the guys and feel pretty sure that they would have made a better go at life than I have.

*　　*　　*

I miss it still. For all the danger, I'll never feel that fearless again. Looking to your left and right and seeing men who will kill and die for you. Who don't have any quit in them. In some ways soldiering is the hardest thing you can do. In some ways it's the easiest. No women. No bills. No responsibilities apart from the job at hand. You know that you can feed yourself and sleep anywhere. In the desert there is nothing you need to catch up on. It's like your life just stopped when you crossed the start line.

You carry yourself with the confidence of indestructible youth. You think you are some righteous force that has been ordained into combat and that you will come out tempered and unscathed. I think sometimes I feel more scared now than I did then. Scared that so much is behind. Back then life rolled out in front of me like a promise.

I cannot imagine ever feeling as alive again. When the bullets were going over my head. You could speak to someone that had done long hard tours and seen terrible things and their nostalgia for those times would be less than mine. But if you ask any soldier if there were any times when they enjoyed it, they could only nod.

You can hazard no greater possession than your own life. No money, no position, no possession can ever be risked with such an absolute finality. There is no way back from that. The greater the risk, the greater the rush that comes from embracing it. There is a terrible draw to gambling so high.

Being a marine gave me a pride and purpose that I have not found since. I would say that it was the time in my life when the challenges to my body and my mind were greatest. In life, satisfaction from completing any endeavour will always be commensurate with what it cost you.

And being a soldier is not just about war. The strongest memories have nothing to do with combat. I saw wonderful things.

In Afghanistan we would do resupplies out of Bagram. When you were underway the loadmaster would tie you in and let you inch forward and dangle your legs over the tail lift. You could edge out there and sit with only sky beneath you. You were close to the gun if you needed to man it, but you never did. Mostly it was just a funfair ride. Your calves were buffeted by the air as you swung from valley to valley. Your stomach would roll at the crests and falls as you would edge over rises and swing down reentrants.

You would see brown faces under black turbans, hands up to shield their eyes from the sun like a salute. You would see goats galloping in terror. We never saw any guns. It was early then. In Bamyam we saw what was left of the Buddhas. Holes and blasted rock in the valley. Desecrated idols. In Bagram they still had the rotten shells of abandoned Soviet fighter planes like the scarred and riddled totems of a burial ground. We did not see the truth in them then. I see it now.

We would sit out on old buildings and watch the sun drop down over snow-frosted peaks before the night came. We would look through our sights and see the greengrained shimmer of a mine-laden wasteland.

In Umm Qasr at the end of Iraq we were waiting in a hangar, cot beds lined out in neat rows. Someone cracked one of the little chemical lights you use to mark out objectives and threw it across the room. Someone cracked another and threw them both back. So it went.

If someone was in the firing line they could not avoid the plastic missiles bouncing around their bed space so they joined in. Ducking incoming. Throwing them back as fast as they could peel off the plastic wrappers. I was in the middle of the hangar lying on my bed and the ceiling came alive. Red, blue, green, yellow. A rainbow of colours shooting back and forward across the sky.

They were arcing above me and so I lay back and watched. You could see an explosion of colours against the black curve of the metal hangar roof. Slow, lazy tracer. We would take the nothing we had and turn it into something.

In the desert there was no need to put on a blanket or a sleeping bag. Just tilt back your head and go to sleep under skies bright with stars. I will never see a sky like it again. Shooting stars arcing across the firmament so often you forget a time when they seemed extraordinary. Satellites tracking slowly across the sky. Absolute silence.

On ships I would set my alarm and go down to the smoking bay at dawn. Behind the safety netting you could smell fuel. The roar of the engines made every conversation a shouting match. But on your own in the twilight all you could see was flat water for miles as you smoked a cigarette down to the embers. Orange and blue above the obsidian of the water as you watched the stars die and the day be born again.

In the night sometimes when you took off layers you could hear the crackles of static and see a dull green phosphoresce around your body. In forestry blocks it was so black it felt like blindness and this emerald glow would wash around you like a shroud.

It is these snapshots in time that I remember most. The sights and sounds that are lost to me now and I will not see again.

What I took with me was endurance and perspective. It is lonely on a long march. All you can see is the pack of the man to your front. When you're so close to the edge that putting one foot in front of the other takes all you have everything else goes out from your mind. You find peace in that place.

Most bad things in your life seep into the empty gaps of time you have. It was sometimes a blessing to have none. On the tough days there was a long grind of constant pressure—to clean, to drill, to learn, to practice. Rest was hard won and sleep was instant.

It gave me a sense of perspective that I will never lose. All the petty degradations give you a tolerance and a patience. I've been shaking with cold in a trench, hungry and tired with no end in sight. Every better day after that feels like a gift.

You learn that you do not go to war for Queen and country. You do it for the men by your side. Someone said it was going to work every day with your best friends and doing the best job in the world. In time, the romance faded. But for a period in my life that was true. And that's a rare thing to find.

Patrick McIlroy

Dead Time
i.m. Fish

Jolted out of the present,
as my grey corporate commute
belatedly winds its way,
seemingly against the odds,
towards its Waterloo,
slow-primed to launch
its sardine-packed battalion
of news-stale,
discordant souls into the mire
of another dull winter's day—

I see you, just, half-hidden,
buried beneath cluttered memories
of near-forgotten times,
tangled together in the dead of a ditch,
as once we were
on that moonlit night on Woodbury,
gorse-cut and snared, sweat-drenched,
laughing and out of time,
lost as I was, you found me
and stiffened my resolve.

And then again,
as the Company gathered
in the shadow of that ancient crumbling fort,
a folly to the conceit of men,
testament to the best laid plans
of lost campaigns long gone,
I saw your name
at the foot of that simple wooden cross,
hard etched on brass,
written as it was beneath
the names of others,
all lost, killed in action
not too far from where we stood,
and thought of you.
No laughter then, or now.

Peter Gill

Four Horsemen

THE GRAVES of St Giles' church in the East Devon village of Kilmington face out over the broad valley of the River Axe which coils its way through muddy banks on the final few miles from Axminster to the sea at Seaton. I want to be buried there, in sight of the town where I grew up and deep in British soil which has offered such firm footing over the decades. Where better for the walker to spend what Thomas Hardy, over the border in Dorset, called the 'long cold claytime'?

Village churchyards are full-up these days and burials often restricted to parishioners. In Kilmington's case, an accommodating landowner has already allowed an ecclesiastical land-grab or two down towards the river. So space is not the immediate problem. I can next point to the graves of my sister, parents, grandparents and uncles already there, some up close to the church. But you still have to apply for a special faculty at a church court in Exeter and for that you need the backing of the parish. Here the vicar made a request on behalf of his parish council. They would like to get to know me a bit better while I was alive, and asked if I would come and speak to them about the life of a foreign correspondent. That was a fair exchange, and this was the theme to which I kept returning.

Wars make the biggest headlines and lead the news bulletins, so where the soldiers are is the first place the ambitious reporter needs to be. But troops move on or move through; they pull back or they advance; they hold their ground or they withdraw; and it is civilians who end up paying the price. Shelling and bombing create the din, but when I think of this reporter's wars it is the silences that stay in the mind. In the commotion of conflict, you know to duck or to hide or to

23

high-tail it out of there. The quiet is more chilling. You know there is danger, but you cannot identify where it is.

In Vietnam and Cambodia in the 1970s, we took taxis to the front, but when the traffic ran out, we had to get out and walk. We might have been told there were friendly troops up ahead, but we could never be sure. They might be dug in by the side of the road or they might be off somewhere in the jungle. Civilians fleeing the fighting passed us on the narrow highways, suggesting we still had a way to go. When there were no more civilians trying to escape, the menace of silence became oppressive.

One Sunday afternoon in Phnom Penh, for no very good reason, I took the old ferry across the Mekong so I could walk the jungle path by the river and look back at a city under siege. Perhaps the idea was as simple-minded as to see what Khmer Rouge gunners saw as they shot up the cargo boats struggling up from Saigon to try and lift the siege. After a few hundred metres there was no one else on the path, and yet I was certain, utterly convinced, that I was being watched, not just by one but by many pairs of eyes. Unlike some journalists at the time, snatched and never seen again, I returned with self-conscious lack of hurry to the ferry and back across the river. Safety is territorial: known ground where nothing is out of sight, everything apparent and on the surface.

Wars deprive civilians of their independence and their capacity to feed themselves. Fighting forces people off their land and turns them into refugees under canvas, provided always that someone has thought of putting up the tents. In Africa's modern wars, there is often little physical separation between the sides, but the land all around is over-populated with casualties—poor people driven to flight and soon enough into hunger. War may be the first horseman, but famine, pestilence and death itself ride in immediately behind.

Of all the nondescript towns in the world, Korem in the Ethiopian highlands will for ever be associated with starvation. There was no front line and there were no trenches in the long war between Tigrayan rebels and the Marxist government of Ethiopia, but Korem offered a measure of security in rebel-run terrain. After successive crop failures and with local trading at a halt, the only option for the hungry was to try and make it to the town. They came from all around, tens of thousands of them walking for days, and there they waited either to be fed or to starve to death.

This was the Ethiopian famine of 1984, the great hunger that reinvented the pop singer Bob Geldof as a forceful and eloquent campaigner. It led to Band Aid and Live Aid and a host of other initiatives that still, more than thirty years on, underpin the rich world's response to the world's poor. At the root of it was not the weather or the wretched harvests. It was the war.

In October that year, I was the first journalist in months to reach Korem. The government exercised rigid control over media movements out of the capital, but sympathetic Ethiopian relief officials calculated that a TV documentary team would look a bit further than the distended bellies of the hungry and so closed their eyes to our departure. In Korem the facts still spoke for themselves.

The young official in charge of the famine relief camp outside the town wore a black jacket and carried a black exercise book under his arm. In this he kept a careful record of life and death in the camp, including the number of people dying of hunger and disease on first a monthly and then on a daily basis. Up to March 1984, he pronounced, the death toll was below a hundred a month; in April because of a fresh influx of the destitute it shot up to 854; six months later on the day I arrived the figure for deaths in the previous twenty-four hours had topped a hundred for the first time.

At the heart of the Korem camp were long tin shelters where the worst of the starvation cases were brought. Children with their mothers and families in some, adults in others. These were the new arrivals, weakened by lack of food and dehydrated by lack of water to the point of collapse. With their saline drips and stethoscopes, foreign and local aid workers had just a few hours to try and revive them. They worked briskly and efficiently and without apparent drama. What characterised this place in the middle of a guerrilla war was again the eeriness of the silence.

The hours around dawn were the time when the TV crew needed to be on station outside the shelters. Now the sound was of keening women grouped around the shrouded corpses of their loved ones. All had been dressed for burial overnight. Since the special homespun for shrouds had run out, many were covered in the rags they wore in life. There were child corpses among them, far too many, some with siblings in wretched little family groups, a few placed alongside a shrouded parent, one child even nestling between both its parents. The burial parties would place the shrouded remains on stretchers and set off at a trot on these final journeys.

Thirty years ago the news compulsion meant sticking to the camp and trying to work out what was needed from back in Europe to cut the death toll and to offer hope to the starving. It was around the twenty-fifth anniversary of the famine that I returned to Ethiopia to survey the topography of a catastrophe which had cost the lives of more than 600,000 people in Korem and across the North. The Tigrayan guerrilla fighters of 1984 were now the government, and that meant that the Tigray Region was favoured with generous investment. Even the weather had been kind to Tigray in recent years. 'Korem was known throughout the world as a town of famine and hunger,' said a solemn local official. 'Now it is a town of development.'

Instead of parched bare earth, there was a flush of green on the plain where the famine camp had stood. Long-horn cattle were grazing there some four months into the dry season. The camp area is bisected by a gully that in 1984 was a bone-dry hazard. Today a little river was flowing through it. In one corner of the site there was a primary school, and the old camp pharmacy, properly built to keep the medicines safe, had become an adult skills centre. Geldof's charity Band Aid was starting work on a hospital, now complete, to give concrete expression to the nearby memorial, 'In Honour of the Children that perished let us build the health of those who follow.'

Where were all the victims of the famine buried then, I asked? My guides gestured in several directions—the Muslims over there, on the other side of the main road, the Christians up ahead near the church at Adi Golo and the cholera victims in a deep communal pit right over there—just behind my hotel. We set off in a pick-up to tour the sites. The Muslim graves were plain mounds of earth, some with a cactus flowering on top, most simply smothered in scrub. In their anonymity, the lime-covered cholera corpses received the least recognition. The Christians, comprising the largest number of dead, were at least taken towards St Mary's at Adi Golo, even though very few came close to the church.

'Better to die than to be buried at Adi Golo,' runs a Tigrayan expression coined in 1984. The point is plain. So undignified, so shaming was the business of dying in the huge famine camp outside Korem that it was surely better to stay at home and forgo the chance of survival altogether. Only locals from Korem itself, not those who had trekked for days to find food there, were given a proper funeral or allowed to be buried in consecrated ground around the church. The rest ended up at the bottom of the hill with no funeral rites beyond a dug grave.

Some famine victims did not even get that. At the worst of these times so many were dying each day that the government started ordering farmers to leave their fields and dig graves instead. They were paid, reasonably enough, on the number of bodies they buried each day. One consequence, witnessed by outraged residents in Adi Golo, was that five, six, sometimes as many as ten bodies were buried in one plot and the gravediggers split the extra fees between themselves.

I walked around the graves at the bottom of the hill. There were no names, nothing recorded for posterity. Most were represented by the modest mound of a filled grave, and that was steadily diminishing with the years to flat earth again. Yet for some an individual effort had been made all that time ago. It took the form of lumps of black volcanic clinker washed out of the soil by the rains. These clinkers had been collected and placed on top of the graves, even arranged in something of a pattern. Was that scattered pile actually a cross?

The road I travelled to Ethiopia in 1984 started in neighbouring Sudan where I was once a volunteer teacher. I began exploring the country and the region and knew I had to return. I still have the cutting from the *Guardian* which helped me on my way. It is dated September 16, 1967, and covers the conflict between Sudan's northern Arab Muslims and southern African Christians and animists. That struggle had already been under way for more than a decade when I visited and it continued for many decades more. Now South Sudan is an independent country, but the vanity of its new leadership and intertribal warfare have made things gravely worse. Today it presents the world with one of its grimmest humanitarian emergencies.

Civilians in South Sudan are more than the accidental victims of conflict. They are its deliberate targets. Southern leaders exploit and inflame the loyalty of their tribespeople and set them against rival communities. This has been the pattern for decades. They go further by punishing and depriving women and children of food when their sole offence is the wrong ethnicity. I made a TV film in the 1980s which we called 'Where Hunger is a Weapon', and that experience brought me face to face with the deadly unexpectedness of guerrilla warfare.

We had to film on both sides of this civil war: in towns held by the northern government; with rebels in the bush. Against a pitiful background of starving children, the southern military governor said to me, 'We will let you know who are the ordinary civilians' and then added, 'In a fighting area the civil population is part of the war. In any place where there is a war the civilian population doesn't get away with it.' The corresponding charge against the rebel leader Col. John Garang was that he was preventing relief flights reaching starving people on the government side by threatening to shoot down the aircraft with the food. 'Something is being hidden,' he said. 'A plane that goes to Wau, purporting to be carrying relief supplies, and could be carrying something else.'

The journey to find John Garang on the Boma Plateau took twenty hours of driving through scrubland and water courses, sometimes getting stuck up to the axles in wet, black cotton soil. It was on the return journey, at the end of all our filming, that one of the intimate disasters of war overtook us. We were in two old Landcruisers, the only vehicles we could hire in neighbouring Kenya to get us to the interview. The second vehicle was fifty yards behind me, heavier than mine because it carried all the camera gear.

There was an explosion. We stopped, got out and looked back. A plume of dirty black smoke rose above the acacia trees in the still afternoon air. The vehicle was round the corner and we set off at a run. We had been having trouble with that Landcruiser. Had the engine finally blown up? It had of course hit a landmine—Soviet manufacture, planted by rebels who were acting as our escorts on this journey but intended to destroy government vehicles. My talented and determined producer Alan Stewart, who was sitting with the equipment in the back, died a while after the explosion and a guerrilla soldier escort was badly injured.

Such was the enormity of this event that panic, even anxiety, played no part in our response. Our other escort, a young rebel officer, had fled the scene, so we had to make do on our own. We tried to care for Alan in his last moments; we reassured the shocked and bruised; we drove for help in the remaining vehicle, but found very little; but we picked up every last battered can of film so that we had something to show for it all. We then squeezed everyone into the remaining vehicle, including Alan in a zipped-up sleeping bag, and we drove the six hours back to the Kenyan border.

A rapid tropical dusk was descending as we left the scene of the explosion. There was no big crater, just a patch of blackened soil on the dirt road. The cab of the vehicle had been blown twenty feet from the passenger compartment. Tyres, wheels and unidentifiable scraps of metal were strewn in between. Twisted camera gear and battered silver boxes lay where they were. We made no effort at all to tidy up. It could be left where it was and to the evocative silence of war.

Gordon Campbell

Empty Quarter

THE ANTIQUITY of the Arab world is most apparent in the south-west corner of the Arabian peninsula, in the arc that begins in Abha (in the mountains of Saudi Arabia) and extends through Yemen with its thousands of ancient earthen buildings (now rapidly disappearing) to Salalah, the Omani seat of the frankincense trade. Many years ago I flew in a series of stages from Jeddah to Salalah. The first stop, in a venerable Tupolev owned by Yemen Airlines, was just over the border at a desert airstrip near Sa'dah, where we refueled. As the fuel was being pumped in, passengers and crew stood in a semi-circle around the fuel pump. Smoking appeared to be compulsory, and the thought of an explosion seemed not to cross anyone's mind as lighters were drawn from pockets.

Eventually I arrived in Salalah, where I had planned to give a lecture and visit regional government officials. On arrival I was met by my host, who explained that my programme had been cancelled. It was New Year (1 Muharram, not 1 January), which had been declared the previous evening when one man whose honesty was attested by two just men had sighted the new moon. New Year is not a holiday in most parts of the Arab world (including Saudi), but unknown to me and my host, it is a holiday in Oman. As it wasn't certain that the moon would be spotted the previous evening, the government had taken the pre-emptive step of declaring a two-day holiday. That meant that my lecture and all appointments had been cancelled.

My host was apologetic, and wanted to know what I would like to do. I proposed going off on my own the next day, and on the day after that, we agreed to go into Ar Rub' al-Khali, the Empty Quarter. On day one I hired a car and went to see the tomb of Job (Nabi Ayoub in the Islamic tradition) on Jebel Ittin. The tomb is about thirteen feet long, as Job was a tall chap. Nearby a huge footprint left by Job is preserved. On the way back to Salalah I paused in a village to buy frankincense and myrrh for my children (good for Christmas pageants in primary schools), and stopped again because a camel had decided to have a nap on the road. As I arrived on the scene, the driver of the car in front of me was kicking the camel, who eventually stirred into life and wandered off. In the early evening I spent several hours watching weaver birds construct their nests. The gentleman weaver builds a nest, and the lady of his heart's affection comes to inspect it. She usually finds it wanting, whereupon the gentleman destroys the nest in a frenzy. He then builds another one, and the process continues until she declares the proposed accommodation to be satisfactory.

The next day I was collected by my host in a 4WD, in which we stored three spare tyres and a jerry can of petrol. The rule is that two vehicles going into the desert can travel alone, but that one vehicle must have a guide. We therefore drove about forty miles across the gravelled southern rim of the desert to the site that Ranulph Fiennes argues (not without reason, but not conclusively) is Ubar, Ptolemy's Atlantis of the Sands. There we collected a friendly Bedu (with rifle), who refused to take any money from us because we were English. He turned out to be one of Fiennes' excavators, and his photograph is in Fiennes' book on *Atlantis of the Sands*. The site is now a large pit, but our new companion described how as a child he had stood at the top of what was then an isolated desert well as his father clambered down to retrieve water. That sense of isolation is now lost, not least because the Omani government has built a group of bungalows at the site, in an attempt to settle the Bedouin. The houses were all unoccupied.

As we were about to leave the gravel for sand, I noticed a small spherical geode, perhaps six inches in diameter, and stopped to collect it. On returning to England I managed to have it cut in half, so exposing its hollow interior, veined with elegant crystalline shapes. It sits on my desk as I write, and is powerfully evocative of my journey. We drove for a few hours into the high dunes, and, like good tourists, climbed a dune, our feet sinking a few inches into the hot sand. I was surprised to see a woody shrub (*calligonum crinitum*) growing on the slopes, as I had assumed that the area would be void of life, but was pleased that shrubs, unlike their counterparts in the Libyan sector of the Sahara, were not accumulating plastic bags that had blown across the desert from distant towns.

I was also intrigued that the dunes all had names; we thinking of them as constantly shifting, but in fact they move very slowly, like desert glaciers.

Our excursion was complete, and I assumed that we were going to return to drop off our guide. He asked, however, if we would mind stopping off to see one of his friends on the way back, and we readily agreed. After driving across the apparently trackless desert for an hour or so, navigating by the dunes, we arrived at a well (wells have been drilled at intervals right across the desert). I am not sure whether we were in Oman or Saudi, as the border is not marked, but that was not a matter for concern. The well was marked by a hut and a water tank, the latter about six feet by ten, and raised about four feet off the ground. It was surrounded at a respectful distance by about thirty camels, many of them black. Beneath the water tank two men (one Arab, one South Asian) sat on a carpet, and we joined them. It was hot (52 C, 126 F), but the shade of the water tank made it bearable. We were given tea that seemed to have been made the previous week, and cigarettes that made me think that my sleeve was burning.

Introductions were effected, and the South Asian man was intro-duced as the slave of the Arab. Their talk was entirely cordial, so the relationship startled me. The slave turned out to be Pakistani, and he had been sold by his father. I was struggling with his language, but my best guess about what he was saying was that the family had arrived in Jeddah for hajj, and the son (now a late middle-aged man) had been sold to raise money for the return journey for the rest of the family. Saudi abolished slavery in 1962 (and Oman in 1970), so the transaction had probably been legal. I had become accustomed to images of slavery that live on in the region. In airports I had on occasion seen a procession of Bengali labourers holding a string as they were led through an airport, and wondered about the extent to which that practice differs from processions of slaves in neck irons. But this man had been a real slave, and that strikes even more powerfully than do evocations of a slavery that has been safely consigned to the past.

In subsequent conversation the slave was largely silent, in part because of the subject of our talk, but also, perhaps, because he only spoke when asked to do so. We learnt that the slave was a permanent resident of the hut, and that his owner visited from time to time to ensure that all was well with his camels. As far as I could tell, the camels served no useful purpose beyond asserting the wealth of their owner, but that could be construed as a useful purpose.

Our host wanted to know what two Brits were doing in Rub' al-Khali. I remarked that we were not the first, and that Englishmen had first crossed the desert in the 1930s. Our guide nodded, and said that his grandfather had worked in the base camp of Sheikh Abdullah al-London. This was Harry St John Philby (father of Kim), who had crossed the Empty Quarter in 1932. The grandfather had not been in the crossing party, but had known Sheikh Abdullah.

This remark prompted our host to speak. His grandfather, he explained, had been with Bertram al-London. I struggled with the name, but my colleague, whose Arabic was much better than mine and who caught the allusion, explained that it was Bertram Thomas (from Bristol, as it happens, but London is England in those parts), who had made the first European crossing in 1930–31, calculating (correctly) that the ensuing book (*Arabia Felix*) might sell well enough to enable him to live comfortably thereafter. Again, our host's grandfather had not been on the crossing, but had been on a side-trip into Yemen. Finally, I mentioned Wilfred Thesiger. Neither our host nor our guide was associated with Thesiger's crossings in the late 1940s, but both recalled that he had visited in the early 1970s, when he had stopped at a well some miles from where we were sitting. It was an extraordinary conversation. I had assumed that the emptiness of the Empty Quarter precluded the notion of any literary dimension, and yet our improbable quintet were sitting in the shade of a water tank while the names of Philby, Thomas and Thesiger floated in the desert air.

In the European imagination the desert is thought of as dead ground, but of course it is alive with xerophytic plants and a range of insects and reptiles. Vestigial numbers of larger animals (Arabian oryx, ostrich, Arabian tigers) were occasionally observed in the desert as late as the 1930s, but thereafter retreated into memory. The oryx survived only in captive populations, but these were sufficient for it to be reintroduced in the 1980s; the ghost of the desert oryx has thus been clothed in flesh. The desert is an extreme meeting place of the visible and the invisible. It offers refuge to human beings, not in the form of cover, but at the bounds of endurance, within the structures of tradition and lore. But in my mind it is vivified above all by the writings of European travellers, even though their narratives are not wholly untainted by colonial assumptions.

Philby, Thomas and Thesiger all spoke Arabic and all dressed as Beduoin when they were in the desert (as did Doughty, Lawrence and others before them). On one reading their clothing was a commendable shedding of colonial dress, but on another there is an element of self-fashioning redolent of seventeenth-century aristocratic ladies dressing as shepherdesses for their portraits. As this generation of Arabists returned from the desert to regale their clubland friends with their exploits, they conjure up images of Buchan's Sandy Arbuthnot with his disguises and effortless command of languages, or Aubrey Herbert, who spoke Turkish, Arabic, Greek, and Albanian, dressed as a tramp, and boasted of having been twice offered the throne of Albania. In thinking of the desert through the filter of such figures, was I complicit in the colonial attitudes that they represented?

We stood to go, as did our host and his slave. I hugged our host, who was benign in his farewells, and shook hands with the slave (South Asians don't hug in such circumstances), who wished me a happy journey. It was a wholly cordial encounter in a social atmosphere that felt entirely peaceful. I knew in my heart, however, that it was the false peace of conquest. Tacitus quotes the Scottish chieftain Calgacus to the effect that in their brutal conquest the Romans had made a desert and called it peace (*ubi solitudinem faciunt, pacem appellant*). The notion of the eternal peace of the desert is of course an illusion. Rub' al-Khali is now the safe space of Al-Qaeda in the Arabian Peninsula, and the escape route of Yemeni criminal gangs operating in Saudi and the Gulf States.

The encounter has stayed vividly with me over the years, partly because of the literary associations, and partly because of the reminder that slavery still exists. It need not be cruel (people can be kind to animals and servants and children), but there is never any question of the unevenly empowered relationship, and the cutting off of life choices is deeply troubling. For all I know, the slave may well still be camel-minding in Ar Rub' al-Khali, enjoying occasional visits from his master, who brings food. The memory serves to remind me that the Quarter is not empty, nor its dead ground, dead.

Brian Turner

Smoking with the Dead and Wounded

FOR MANY YEARS, I practiced the art of dying. During my enlistment as an active duty infantryman in the U.S. Army, I died more times than I can remember. I was blown up by a simulated hand grenade inside a mock village at Camp Rilea, on the Oregon coast. A sniper killed me as the snow fell in Fort Drum, New York. Heavy machine-gun fire cut me down just beyond a breach in the wire during a predawn assault of a mock city in Fort Lewis, south of Puget Sound. I was wiped out during an in-defilade defense, along with my entire platoon, as we fought for several hours in the California desert country of Fort Irwin—attempting to hold off a Soviet-styled regimental punch-through of our brigade perimeter, replete with mine sappers, attack helicopters modified to look like Russian Hinds, BMPs, tanks, and a company of follow-on infantry. At the Yakima Training Center in eastern Washington, a squad of infantry hunted me down and shot me as I crawled in the dead grasslands high up on a ridge.

I died until death became a way of life for me.

* * *

And I can tell you this: the dead smoke unfiltered Camels when they can get them. They sit in the back of a two-and-a-half-ton cargo truck as it rolls and bounces down a red clay road at the U.S. Army's Joint Readiness Training Center (JRTC) in Fort Polk, Louisiana. It's mid afternoon and humid, even in November 2002, and Vasquez, a stocky sergeant from Texas and a well-liked NCO in the battalion, recounts the story of how he was wounded a few hours back. Some of the soldiers laugh as they lean forward on the bench to hear him better, but I've drifted off into the cloud of dust forming and re-forming in our wake, framed by stands of longleaf and blackjack pine, a gray ceiling of cloud overhead, impending rain.

Of course, I'm not sure how much laughing there'd be if this were the real deal. All of us have been given cards detailing wounds received on the battlefield. Head wounds, sucking chest wounds, abdominal bleeding caused by shrapnel, legs shot of from under us, concussions. If this were the real deal, I'd be zipped up in a body bag and lying on a hard metal bed. And Sgt. Vasquez might ask someone for a smoke, but I doubt he'd tell stories of how he'd made it out while the dead lay in black bags at his feet. I imagine him holding an I.V. bag up for the soldier next to him, the way the medic showed him, maybe closing his eyes for a time, exhausted.

For now, though, all of us wear a webbing of sensors over our uniforms. These sensors are made specifically for force-on-force field exercises, and they emit a high-pitched *beep beep beep* when one of us has been shot or wounded; those of us who get a long and uninterrupted flatlining sound immediately know we've been killed on the spot. Like several others in the truck bed, I'd been handed a small white card on the battlefield that announced, in bold-faced, 24-point Times New Roman font: KIA. *Killed in Action.* The OC (Officer in Charge, who is similar to a referee in sports) used a small metal key to turn off the sound bleeding from my equipment. I took a breath, dusted myself off, and began walking to the nearest dirt road. I also began to think about this process of dying, the efficiency of it all akin to that of a factory floor working 24/7, and how the war itself simply moved on without me, a kind of wave that rolled back out to sea.

* * *

So it is with the dead. There's time to think. Time to measure the choices made, options discarded—all that was done weighed against the vast assembly of what was once possible. In actual combat, like the looming war in Iraq that we're training for in the semitropical landscape of the

American South, I wonder if convoys transport the dead to processing tents somewhere beyond the sound of artillery and small-arms fire. Are there Mermite cans filled with rice and chicken, Army coffee waiting at the end of the road? And what about the civilians who've died on the battlefield, the wounded children marooned in their pain, those left to wail under the shade of a leafy pine? I've watched the OPFOR, the enemy, rise from their deaths to dust themselves off before beginning the slow walk toward their former lives. The resignation in their bearing cannot fully veil the fact that they will return tomorrow, or next week, or next month, iteration by iteration, one battle after another, until they've pulled the trigger and killed as many as their bullets allow.

Who mourns for them? Who writes letters to their loved ones and who delivers the news? Who will come to carry their bodies from the field?

* * *

When I died in Regensburg, a mock city in Fort Drum, I untangled myself from a coil of concertina wire and lay with my back on the cold, wet ground, my breath ghosting from my mouth as I listened to the fighting roll on into the buildings and lanes of the town. I thought about the original 10th Mountain Division soldiers—my ancestors—when they first conducted training before shipping overseas against the Nazis. I imagined them low-crawling between the trees around me. One of them, maybe a rancher from Colorado, or a lumberman from Alaska, paused to look at me for a moment before digging his elbows into the frigid earth and moving forward.

In Fort Lewis, when our platoon was obliterated in an artillery barrage after we'd dropped ramps from our vehicles and run into the tree line, an OC walked up and pointed out each man who'd died— saying *you* and *you* and *you* and, *over there, you, yeah you*. I imagined the dead from the Vietnam era among the shadows in the trees further up the slope of the hill. They smoked and said not a word. Now and then one of them would stand and slowly work his way down the hill to us, his body backlit in sunlight, his shadowy form leaning over to offer a hand and help us to our feet.

And so it is with the dead. They offer a smoke and lift each other up, point the way to the nearest road, start walking.

*   *   *

In Louisiana, we drive from one collection point to another as Barnes, sitting shoulder-to-shoulder with me by the tailgate, asks about going to helicopter school when we return to garrison. We talk about this, and about his wife and kids, as the truck lurches to a stop outside the main processing tent: Mortuary Affairs.

Sgt. Vasquez stands in the truckbed and mimes blowing a dramatic kiss to us as the wounded laugh and drive off to wherever the wounded go. We file into the tent, handing our KIA cards to a skinny kid in a uniform that looks about one size too big for him. He points to a table with coffee and a stack of Styrofoam cups, and tells us to help ourselves.

Take your time, I think. I just want to sit propped up against the green duffle bags in the back corner with the rest of the dead. I want to be forgotten for a while. Drink some lukewarm coffee, lean my head back, and get some solid rack time. There's time enough for the paperwork at Graves Registration and for the short walk over to the In-Processing tent —where fresh soldiers arrive green from the world after being requisitioned by a unit short on bodies. For now, I don't want to ponder the strange reincarnation I am undergoing, this cycling back to war. I want to sit here and rest among the dead. Let Barnes snore with his machine gun on its bipod beside him. Let Parazoo read *Lord of the Rings* one more time. Let Bogans mumble to himself as he writes the words down, working on his 'flow', getting it just right, while somewhere not too far away Sgt. Vasquez lies on an operating table in a cloud of anesthesia as a surgeon from Missouri applies a scalpel and a rotary saw to his breastbone, opening him up before peering into the wound that took Vasquez down.

On the hillside where the OC handed me my KIA card, a black-throated gray warbler sings from somewhere out of view, and then falls silent. The ghost from Vietnam takes a slow drag from an unfiltered Camel. He listens to the crickets in the afternoon grass, that continual background static of the world, and then exhales a long rolling plume of smoke toward the low hollow where I died.

Kate McLoughlin

Fatal Incomprehension

at least you know
How to report on a landscape

Henry Reed, 'Judging Distances'

WAR TRANSFORMS the meaning of landscape. What was pastoral in peacetime becomes threatening in conflict: once benign terrain is now cover for the sniper, the ambush, the mine. Hostile territory is foreign country and its language must be learned like any other foreign tongue. Yet this language has unique challenges. Failing to understand it is potentially fatal, and its acquisition necessitates a specialized way of relating to the environment. This relationship is neither the Romantic view of Nature as a source of truth nor the transcendental understanding of a figure like Thoreau nor yet ecological awareness. Rather it is an animalistic alertness to environs that is as much bodily impulse as cognitive strategy. Two contemporary poets—Isabel Palmer and Brian Turner—appreciate the vital necessity of being able to interpret the war zone in this manner. Palmer writes from the perspective of a mother whose son has been sent to war; Turner from that of a military veteran. The ancient divide between combatant and civilian evaporates in the realization that survival depends upon proficiency in the language of the land.

Isabel Palmer is a British poet whose father and son, both called Harry, served at different times in the Rifles Regiment. The younger Harry was sent to Afghanistan just after his 21st birthday in 2011 and was later deployed to Northern Ireland. In a poem called 'Whatever', Palmer describes, with violent imagery, how she was unable to talk to her son about his mobilization:

> I couldn't find the words
> if someone jammed a screwdriver
> down my throat to twist out
> my swallowed tongue.

In lieu of uttering her true feelings aloud, Palmer sent weekly poems to Harry while he was on active service, a number of which were collected in a pamphlet, *Ground Signs*, in 2014 by the small poetry imprint Flarestack. In 2016, Bloodaxe republished *Ground Signs* (with amendments and additions) as a sequence called *Atmospherics* in *Home Front*, a volume featuring 21st-century war poetry by Palmer and three other women. (In this essay, I am quoting from *Atmospherics*.)

Throughout the sequence, Palmer displays concern about non-comprehension. 'Language Card (Dari)' and 'On Pen Y Fan' complement each other, the former focusing on understanding of language, the latter on knowledge of landscape. 'Language Card (Dari)' took its inspiration from the colour-coded phrasebooks in Dari and Pashto given to British and American soldiers serving in Afghanistan. Conveying both astonishment and fear about the paucity of linguistic information on offer, Palmer works through the words assigned to each colour—'Questions hang violet'; 'child, bomber, thief' are in 'the same shade of pink'; time expressions are in 'poisonous yellow'; 'Orders are red'; 'Small talk is green'—while noting that 'There are no words / for fog, flood, scorch'. How, then, can these phenomena, so important on the battlefield, be communicated? The question is left unanswered. 'Language Card (Dari)' does not so much forge connections across languages as perpetuate divisions.

Compare the worse-than-nothing linguistic knowledge of 'Language Card (Dari)' with the rich understanding of the landscape recorded in 'On Pen Y Fan'. This poem looks back to the other Harry, Palmer's father, who trained commandos on Pen Y Fan, the highest peak in the Brecon Beacons. 'He knew her face', Palmer writes of the elder Harry's relationship with the mountain, and he taught his charges 'how to follow flies / and finches straight and low / to water'. It is knowledge that was fatally lacking on 13 July 2013 when Lance-Corporal Craig Roberts, Lance-Corporal Edward Maher and Corporal James Dunsby died on a sixteen-mile SAS selection march on the mountain. The three army reservists collapsed from heat-related illness, and Palmer concludes her poem with a sentence-long reflection on how her father would have made sure that they knew what they needed to:

> He would have told you
> how the thirsty sun wraps
> you in her spider silk and drinks,
> pours you into shadows
> shredded between rocks
> and turns your spit to soot.

The poem's epigraph is from Sun Tzu's *The Art of War*: 'We are not fit to lead an army unless we are familiar with the face of the country.'

In 'On Pen Y Fan' we glimpse the kind of knowledge necessary for survival in arduous terrain. But this is not quite yet the specialized knowledge of hostile territory which must be acquired rather more quickly than Harry the Elder's deep familiarity with the Welsh mountains. In her poem 'Ground Signs', Palmer moves on to demonstrate the nature of this specialized knowledge, comparing the illegibility of the landscape with the impenetrability of Dari to non-Dari speakers. 'Ground Signs' concerns Harry the Younger's work with a Vallon, a metal detector used widely in Afghanistan to search for Improvised Explosive Devices (IEDs):

Why you?

Not so long ago,
you could lose
keys, batteries, bicycles and limp
home with just one shoe.

'Is there no-one else?' One
who can drop down on his belt buckle
at a sudden shrine
of painted stones, red,
white, *surkh*, *safayd*. Someone

who knows better than to cross a ditch
no wider, on the landing side,
than one soldier's boot,

who sifts the ground signs ankle-deep
in upturned soil, still fresh
in midday sun, at slow-down points
of overlooking, who notes

the shifting sand on wood and track,
the locals out of sight,

the old man's goat left bleeding.

In this situation, foreign in multiple senses of the word, reading has
to be re-learned from scratch. The Vallon is detecting the landscape's
voicings—the 'metal spoor' that lies 'ankle-deep' in the subsoil. But
the poem mentions other, non-metallic signs that also require deci-
phering. What is the meaning of the 'sudden shrine'—who has died
and what might be the consequences? What might the 'out of sight'
locals be avoiding, or observing? What does the old man's bleeding

goat signify; how has it been harmed? These details comprise the unfamiliar vocabulary of the landscape. They are scattered severally, failing to combine syntactically, as the awkward spacings between the stanzas show. Shrine—sand—goat: how do they fit together? This is hypervigilance mirrored in poetic form. The speaking voice of the poem—the soldier's mother—quite reasonably questions whether he is competent to interpret what he sees: 'Why you?' she asks; and, plaintively, 'Is there no one else?'

Interpretative competence can make the difference between life and death in such circumstances—the reference to a foothold 'no wider […] than one soldier's boot' ineluctably brings to mind what would happen if that boot stepped on a booby trap. The Dari words present in the poem—'*surkh*' and '*safayd*'—model the danger since most western readers of the poem will not be familiar with them. (Palmer is treading here in the footsteps of Thomas Hardy who, inserting Afrikaans words into his Boer War poem 'Drummer Hodge' more than a century earlier, showed its readers what it was like to face hostile unfamiliarity, if not to die from it.) Palmer provides their meanings in a glossary at the end of *Ground Signs* (but not *Home Front*), but even without this help the juxtaposition of the words gives the Anglophone reader a hefty clue that *surkh* means 'red' and *safayd* 'white' (the English appears directly beneath the Dari in *Ground Signs*). Yet the non-Dari-speaking reader can't be *absolutely certain* of this. Doubt remains—an instant that dramatizes the inexperienced soldier's doubt. Do things mean what they seem to mean? Is the far side of the ditch safe or dangerous? 'Ground Signs' conveys the fear of not knowing, or of guessing wrongly.

In a poem with a virtually identical title—'Signs'—Palmer repeats the theme. 'Signs' opens with a list of 'Things that mean other things':

> tattoos, cap badges,
> padlocks on lampposts, on garbage bins

Tattoos might have personal meaning; cap badges might be felt to be ironic; padlocks might signify the ever-present possibility of bombs being planted. But besides these there are still 'Other things', lots of them:

> clay bricks, an unsmoked cigar
> beneath a wooden cross, a branch
> tied to a donkey's tail; a boy
>
> who stands too long
> on the cross-hairs of a passing convoy;
> mirror flashes, kites that hang
> on days of rising wind, their feet swaying.

How can sense be made of all these visual clues? Where, for that matter, are we? The presence of the poem in *Ground Signs* gives rise to the assumption that, like the rest of the collection, it is about Afghanistan, but in *Home Front* a location is added as an epigraph—Ballykinler, Northern Ireland, where 2 Rifles were based from 2008 to 2014. 'Signs' also contains a reference to the Ponte Milvio in Rome—the site of a battle in 312 CE. But, whether in Northern Ireland or Afghanistan or ancient Rome, we are told that 'things mean other things'. So what does a branch tied to the tail of a donkey mean? Is it benign or sinister? Why does the boy stand too long? Is he a decoy, a threat, or does the speaker feel worried about his safety? Like 'Ground Signs', 'Signs' gives rise to questions, without providing a framework of meaning within which they can be answered.

The poem concludes:

> So when you see
> that squaddie, who lost his legs,
> whose fingers, on his rifle hand, clung
> to his elbow like scorched fruit,

on his way to the Medals Parade,
his laughter rattling like old bones,
you have to look away.

Ostensibly, these final lines do contain something that the reader can make sense of: we know what it means for a uniformed man to be maimed and we know what medals are awarded for. But the warning of the poem continues: if 'things mean other things', the injuries, the medals and the laughter are pointing to something else—most obviously the attritional effect of armed conflict on human beings. Contrasting with the hypervigilance that the soldier in the war zone must acquire, the observer's impulse is to 'look away'—not to uncover what 'things mean'. 'Signs' itself treads carefully, allowing inferences but not providing definitive meanings for the objects it accumulates. Reading it, one feels wary, alive to ominous possibilities.

Brian Turner faced those possibilities over seven years of military service. An American poet and essayist, he fought in Iraq and Bosnia with the Second Infantry Division of the United States Army. His debut collection, *Here, Bullet* (2005) won a number of awards, and his second collection, *Phantom Noise* (2010) was shortlisted for the T. S. Eliot poetry prize. The opening poem of *Here, Bullet*, 'A Soldier's Arabic', describes a language made of the land itself:

> The word for love, *habib*, is written from right
> to left, starting where we would end it
> and ending where we might begin.
>
> Where we would end a war
> another might take as a beginning,
> or as an echo of history, recited again.
>
> Speak the word for death, *maut*,
> and you will hear the cursives of the wind
> driven into the veil of the unknown.

This is a language made of blood.
It is made of sand, and time.
To be spoken, it must be earned.

This is a careful, guarded, respectful poem. Its use of the pronoun 'we' makes it initially seem as though an antagonistic set of viewpoints will be established—'us' versus 'them'. But this possibility is cancelled: rather than 'they', the speaker simply says that 'another' might think differently. There is more than one way of seeing, that is: one person's end is another person's beginning, just as some languages are written from left to right and others from right to left. Particularly striking is the remark about Arabic in the last line: 'To be spoken, it must be earned'—not *learned*, as one might have expected, but *earned*. Turner articulates the language's history, comprised of 'blood', 'sand' and 'time'. This is not something that can be gleaned from a glossary or grammar: to have the right to speak this tongue requires deep understanding of where things start and finish, of how ownership accrues over time, of the nature and significance of the ubiquitous sand. A soldier's Arabic, that is, will be—should be—the language of the landscape.

Turner's 'What Every Soldier Should Know', from the same volume, has the same theme as Palmer's 'Ground Signs' and 'Signs': the thoroughgoing redefinition process wrought on the environment by war:

> If you hear gunfire on a Thursday afternoon,
> it could be for a wedding, or it could be for you.

> Always enter a home with your right foot;
> the left is for cemeteries and unclean places.

> *O-guf Tera armeek* is rarely useful.
> It means *Stop! Or I'll shoot.*

> *Sabah el khair* is effective.
> It means *Good Morning.*

[…]

There are bombs under the overpasses,
in trashpiles, in bricks, in cars.

[…]

Small children who will play with you,
old men with their talk, women who offer chai—

and any one of them
may dance over your body tomorrow.

There is great cynicism here: Turner is under no illusions about the hatred felt towards the American military forces and the consequential need to develop the capacity to read the landscape for threats. Even if we think that the poem is about genuine connections, about authentically reaching out to those 'small children' and 'old men with their talk' and 'women who offer chai', it is difficult to be sure. In this landscape of misleading signs, the nature of the 'effectiveness' of the polite greeting is ambiguous. It may be that '*Sabah el khair*' is 'effective' because it forges a link between human beings above and beyond their identities as soldiers and civilians. But it may alternatively be 'effective' because it lulls people into a false sense of security, makes them easier to monitor or direct or kill. The whole of 'What Every Soldier Should Know' is an unstable ethical, linguistic and physical landscape in which opposing alternatives are viable at any moment.

War converts the innocent into the threatening. In consequence, landscape requires reappraisal with specialist insight. Trying to convey what it means to acquire such insight, Palmer and Turner suggest that it is something like grappling with a difficult foreign language. As with the Dari and Pashto of Afghanistan and the Arabic of Iraq, odd words and phrases might be recognizable, but syntax—connectivity—is harder to swot up. Details of the landscape are observed individually, that is, but not joined together into a meaningful whole. These poems, full of discontinuous impressions, asking unanswerable questions, mark rather than remedy the fatal incomprehension.

Nicholas Pierpan

The Marine in the Malibu Classic

SOMETIMES, on the road growing up, another driver would give my father the middle finger. Then the US Marine inside him would re-emerge.

Usually my father is a man of quiet patience and control. Even his wilder intensities carry such discipline. He painted our house one summer and then repainted it the exact same colour the following summer. No one ever found out why. He still washes his car every weekend with a precision you do not interrupt. I think having four sons and a messy wife made such things a refuge; he was forced to concede that the inside of his house would be a wreck, but the outside of it could look perfect and he always drew the line at his car.

Such compromises between himself and his family worked pretty well except for the *Malibu Classic*, a wood-panelled station wagon my father bought in 1980. He showed a rare happiness when he got this car brand-new off the lot. It was a big step up from the used clunkers that had preceded it: first a jalopy he had bought for $100 (we were delighted it lasted a year), then a green 70s Chevy Nova (the worst car ever made, not just aesthetically). Now we drove around, stylishly encircled by wood panelling, and everyone had a place to sit. My father had left the Marines years before and was going to night school to earn a law degree. There was a wonderful, American feeling that the impossible was becoming possible. And my father really is a very good driver. Everything happens with uncanny steadiness—the way he brakes for a light, or takes a turn—always the same way, at the same speed.

Except when another driver gave my father the middle finger amid some contested moment of traffic. This gesture, in America at least, is more than rude. It explicitly dares you to do something about it, when any meaningful response massively ups the stakes. There is really nowhere to take things except violence. For my father, any retaliation at all was incongruous given the station wagon he now drove. Maybe young headbangers and toughies saw him looking nicely suburban, and so an easy mark for sticking their chests out. And these moments would have been good ones for my father to compromise—accept his new, wood-panelled family life and let it slide, like any upwardly-mobile person should.

But he never did. I would be daydreaming in the back and feel abrupt jolts of acceleration. Protests from my mother to 'just let it go' always received the same curt reply: 'He gave me the bird.'

'The bird' is what my father has always called the middle finger. I don't know why. It is not commonly-used. I've often wondered if that is what the Marines call it, and if retaliating to the bird is an essential part of boot camp. Our wood-panelled station wagon would soon be chasing muscle cars, or even pert little sports cars, down crowded highways. If the driver got cut off by my father or frozen in traffic, my father would get out. I saw him lean into one window and say, 'Do that again and I'll rip that finger off your hand'. Such threats were not the silly bravado of professional wrestlers. Other men—especially young men who fancied themselves 'tough'—could see my father was ready to go all the way, and it scared them. They were never really confronted with that in normal life.

We knew this kind of thing came from my father's previous life as a Marine. The link once came out overtly when a family friend down the street, Rob, was having a problem: neighbourhood louts had begun sitting on a low wall across his road, drinking and carrying on until the early hours. They were keeping Rob's children awake. He politely asked them to stop gathering there but had been roundly ignored, so Rob wanted to confront them. He rang my father to provide some support. As my mother was out, my father had to bring my older brother and me along. It could not have been very intimidating to see my bespectacled father walking down the street with his eleven year-old and seven year-old in tow, but we were the backup.

On the wall a few men and women drank and smoked, young but well past adolescence. Rob told them to leave. He met disregard, then resistance. My father got involved and somehow took the lead. He was head-to-head with one of the men, who said he was going home to fetch his gun, then come back and shoot my father. My father responded by pounding his finger into his own chest and shouting 'Here—you shoot me *right here*. I was in Vietnam and I'll fucking kill you.'

If those words seem odd or even ridiculous on the page, they boomed down the street. We never saw that man, or any of the others, again.

My father was not someone who often mentioned his time in Vietnam or the Marines. Such moments stand out because they were so rare. I knew he had believed in the war, believed he'd had a solemn duty to serve—whether he liked the war or not—and had done so: he was a Marine from 1966 to 1971, did his tour in 1969–1970, and had never really intended to make the military a career. That was it. To try to make any more out of it risked scorn or, more typically, he'd just ignore you. Focusing on our life now, or the life we were supposed to be living, was much better.

But uncomfortable echoes still pierced that new, suburban normality my parents spent all their waking hours trying to afford. Not long after we moved to Virginia, for example, my father put on a sweatshirt I had never seen before. It had the name of his Marine Corps company on it. My parents packed everyone into the *Malibu Classic* for a surprise trip to Washington, DC. We parked near a vast crowd gathering on the Mall. It was the Dedication Ceremony for the Vietnam Veterans Memorial.

My mother handed me a comic book. I was nine years old and needed something to occupy me during the long course of speeches. I sat down on the grass with a new issue of *G.I. Joe: A Real American Hero*. Its cover showed soldiers in deep arctic snow, brandishing M-16s. One was mischievously blowing bubble gum. A caption read '*Panic at the North Pole!*' The story inside was the perfect combination of danger and inevitable victory. That might sound awful, but such manicured drama was not too far from what I saw on the news that evening. The lead story showed veterans at the ceremony, embracing each other in floods of tears. The newscaster underscored these images with sombre, knowing lines like 'Today, at least… it was all right… for grown men… to cry'.

I saw neither *G.I. Joe* soldiers nor crying vets around me that day. The densely-packed crowd of men in their 30s and 40s looked totally normal, the kind of people you'd see anywhere. Some wore a field jacket or boonie hat on top of civilian clothes. Some had bumper stickers slapped on their backs saying '*USMC*' or '*ARMY*'. A bit of talk rumbled through them, occasional laughter, but mostly a quiet anticipation. Everyone's focus stayed on that distant spot of canvas in the wind. As a child, I felt like we were in a vast queue. Everyone was facing the same direction and just waiting.

But this would not be another Lincoln memorial or Bunker Hill obelisk—typical American monuments built with limestone in Greco-Roman or Egyptian styles. The Vietnam memorial was simple black walls submerged straight into the earth. They carried no established symbols honouring service, courage, or sacrifice. The decorated Vietnam veteran (and soon-to-be Senator) James Webb had publicly objected to this design, saying 'I never in my wildest dreams imagined such a nihilistic slab of stone'. Other prominent voices dubbed it 'a black gash of shame' and even 'a tombstone'.

It is unfair to patronise these anxieties now, knowing the overwhelmingly positive impact the memorial would have. It was 1982 and, with Reagan and a re-ignited Cold War, the military was finally heroic again in the public eye. Maybe the square-jawed super-warriors of *G.I. Joe* were still a step too far, but for many the memorial's design seemed like a dark step backwards.

At one point this collision, between new Reagan pride and 'dead ground' of the recent past, came to the fore. On the podium a woman gave a rousing speech of old-school patriotism. 'And if we need to…' she said at the end, 'GOD DAMN IT WE'LL DO IT AGAIN!' Cries of support did not carry the crowd. The people around me bristled in soundless reproach. As ordinary as these people looked, there was something cogent about them that I couldn't quite name.

There were later processions and marching bands that did not carry this crowd, either. Something was going on that I was only starting to grasp, far from both *G.I. Joe* and the evening news. But my parents said nothing about the ceremony on the drive home. They were not going to talk about what the memorial or day 'meant', although by then I very much wanted to know. Every child leaves the world of safe, uncomplicated images; this abstract memorial and the crowd I'd seen was something else again. But no one said anything in the *Malibu Classic,* and this is the silence I most remember. I had been left hanging. My father was occupied with his usual driving—hitting the brakes with a perfect steadiness, taking a turn in the same measured way—and as far as I can remember we never mentioned that day again.

Vesna Goldsworthy

Collateral Damage

Throughout the seven years of war
This is how we divide the papers:
You take the news section
I take whatever's left—
Cookery, Fashion, Stars—
So long as there are no columns of refugees
No ancient hatreds, no death,
Nor any of the euphemisms for it.

I don't want you to read the news, I say,
Not at breakfast,
Nowhere near any bread I make;
I don't want you to read the news,
And I don't want the news read to me.

For, sooner or later, the dining table
Divides along ethnic lines.
Your people and my people
Line up behind us
Waving their phantom fists at each other
Whispering: see, this is how it all starts
Not here, not today, but always further back.

The black crater in that picture by your coffee cup,
That startling wound in a street I know,
Like a socket left behind a wisdom tooth.
Our pilots, you say. Do I hear pride?

That *our* which feels no longer *mine*,
That building I won't see again,
That staircase with a row of columns
Which sheltered my first kiss many years ago,
Now a crater full of nothing in a photograph
Leaving a black imprint on your fingertips:
Is there a way to unknow them all?

No collateral damage, you say,
And I concede. Yet a hairline fissure,
Opens and runs with the speed of sound
To connect that nothing and this island,
And stubbornly refuses to heal
Throughout the seven years of war, and after,
Visible only at certain angles and in certain lights.

Christopher Ricks

*'Ground of being
on his ground of escape'*

Arm in arm, my father and I return
to the ground of his failed escape:
it is now forty-eight years on.

'A walk with my father on the Iron Curtain'

Carmen Bugan, poet of Romania. Born, 1970. Came to the United States (with her parents and her siblings), 1989.

NICOLAE CEAUŞESCU, dictator of Romania. Born, 1918. Came to absolute power (with his wife), 1965. Killed, 1989. Disinterred, to be interred afresh, 2010.

Carmen Bugan's well-founded memoir in prose, *Burying the Typewriter* (2012), opened with a poem, 'Visiting the country of my birth'. (In George Herbert's world, such might have constituted for his Temple a threshold, 'Superliminare'.)

The tyrant and his wife were exhumed
For proper burial; it is twenty years since
They were shot against a wall in Christmas snow.

Proper burial not only for the party-leader, but—some years earlier— for the anti-party machine. It had been proper, albeit illegal, to bury the typewriter. (Rather, to bury *a* typewriter, for secretly there was another typewriter that rested not in dead ground but in the living room; unhidden at a plain site; in terms of the hunt, a stalking horse.) 'Proper burial' as prudent, then. The authorities, finding the typewriter to be incriminating evidence of dissidence, would decline to confess that the incriminated party was not the courageous citizen but Ceauşescu and his Communist Party. Carmen Bugan brings all this to book, with photos of the hole dug in the ground and of its contents, alongside the wording of the secret police files (to all of which she has now been given access and to which she accords deeply imaginative resolution in both her memoir and her poems). 'After we lifted the plastic sack we saw in the hole a plastic white container, buried 40 cm deep.'

Burying the … might have moved sharply to *Hatchet*. To lay down one's arms, to cease from hostilities; the resumption of hostilities being to dig up the hatchet. But no.

> Then Father would take the hatchet from behind the stove and
> patrol the house, 'This is my house, no one comes into my
> house, or I'll kill him!' He'd wait with our key placed in the
> door so it couldn't be pushed out.
>
> 'At hour 1:32' *Releasing the Porcelain Birds* (2016)

(The modest comma after *the house*, opening into *my house… my house*, is placed there for—is the key to—the push of mounting realization.)

Father, her father, was imprisoned, tortured. He made an escape but was seized. Secret police: 'The aforementioned objects belong to escapees Bugan Ion and P.T. who crossed the frontier from the People's Republic of Romania to the People's Republic of Bulgaria on the day of 21.02.1965.' But Ceauşescu sought to hold for Romania (in commerce with the United States) the 'most-favored nation' accreditation, so there was to come something of an amnesty.

The dictator released the news of amnesty on his birthday
'To remain in history for his clemency,' Mother said
Not knowing it was her irony that remained preserved:
In our country people starved and friend informed on friend.

'Found in secret police records'

The news was good yet it could not but jar: *amnesty, history, clemency, country*, taking in but moving on from *irony*. Irony that knows the Iron Curtain (and that knows how tellingly askew is the preposition on in 'A walk with my father on the Iron Curtain'). 'Found in secret police records' is in Part I—likewise headed 'FOUND IN SECRET POLICE RECORDS'—of *Releasing the Porcelain Birds*, which bore a subtitle: *poems after surveillance*. There the preposition does double-duty, *after* as the poet's having survived surveillance temporally (not temporarily) as well as the poet's being darkly grateful for a resource of an unexpected kind, unwelcome were it not that art welcomes uglinesses that it can transform. Samuel Beckett translated some 'Maximes' under the title 'Long after Chamfort'.

Better on your arse than on your feet,
Flat on your back than either, dead than the lot.

'Ground of being on the ground of his escape'. The grounds proved anything but dead. Nothing could have been more alive than this ground of being, this profound faith in freedom, honesty, probity (Carmen Bugan, having been shortlisted in 2013, was in 2017 made a Fellow of the Orwell Prize) for which Ion Bugan and his family suffered. Her father's typewriter—the family typewriter whatever the sacrifices and fears within the imperilled family—bequeathed a word-smithy that is now owned by an incorruptible woman of letters. Her words are in open view and in plain hearing for the eyes and ears of people who value every single tongue but not the forked one. 'Preparing for the journey of return' has something to add:

and we have embraced new languages
starting from nothing in the middle of our lives.

That typewriter you planted last year in your garden, has it begun to
sprout? What was planted (not by the secret police, this time) in the
garden in Romania was no corpse. Dead ground within the garden,
possibly, but only as not visible (it was to be hoped) and as not vulnerable from certain vantage-points. The world was supposed not to know
of its existence, this ground of being, with its seasonable miracle of an
unseen inhumed life. George Herbert again, in 'The Flower':

> Who would have thought my shrivelled heart
> Could have recovered greenness? It was gone
> Quite underground; as flowers depart
> To see their mother-root, when they have blown;
> Where they together
> All the hard weather,
> Dead to the world, keep house unknown.

Whereas the hearts of neighbour-informers, fair-weather as against
hard-weather friends, did shrivel, none of the family hearts kept in the
Bugan house (we hear every one of them in these writings) ever shriv-
elled. Yet every heart found itself, at some point, pleading to be shriven.

Since Herbert's day, since those seasons of his, the underground
recovery of 'Dead to the world' has itself had shrivelling visited upon
it. Where it had once compacted its sense into 'seeming, to the unim-
aginative ground-eyed world, to be dead, but no such thing, most truly
alive', this 'Colloq. phr.' *dead to the world* has come since 1899 to mean,
vacantly, 'unconscious or fast asleep; unaware of the external world'.

Unaware is the nub. The death-dealing dangers—and opportuni-
ties—of 'dead ground', in military terminology, are among the things
of which you cannot beware (and of which you cannot avail yourself)
unless you are aware of them. Much as you cannot ignore something
the presence of which you were ignorant of.

The company commander of the present book is going to have
to ensure that his awkward squad doesn't too often iterate—as the
announced foundation—the term dead ground. But it was very quietly
that the *Oxford English Dictionary* directed us (Cf.) from *dead*—

> *Mil.* Denoting an area which cannot be fired on from
> a particular point because of the nature of the ground,
> intervening obstacles, etc. –

where the citations, all of which put 'dead' within quotation marks, are
1899, 1900, and 1919, to *angle*: '(Cf. *dead angle* in D. 2.)'

> Special combs. *dead angle* (*Fortif.*), 'any angle of a
> fortification, the ground before which is unseen, and
> therefore undefended from the parapet', Stocqueler *Milit.*
> *Encycl.* [1853, a date that you have to unearth from the
> dead ground of the OED's *finis*, its Bibliography]

Dead ground is markedly unobtrusive, off there within *dead angle*, but
in the words 'therefore undefended' there is a valuable complication
of the military scene, even as 'cannot be fired on' is crucially different
from, say, 'cannot be surveyed (or surveilled), may not even be recognized as dead ground.' As for that oppositely valuable thing, a simpli-
fication, we can be grateful that, under *dead ground*, one dictionary
reminds us of the altogether usual fact: 'an area of ground hidden from
an observer due to undulations in the land.'

For *undulations* does the trick in bringing home that, when not on
the battlefield, most of us have to beware of dead ground only when
we are at the wheel. Is it safe, at this very moment, to overtake (or be
overtaken)? We can't see what may be hiding within dead ground; we
may not have known or seen that there *is* dead ground. And what with
licensed rage and all, haven't roads become battlefields, lethally alive
with open hostilities that can make the worst of dead ground? Here
the masterpiece was created not by words alone but by the antagonisms
and co-operations of different media that constitute the art of film:
Steven Spielberg's road-raging *Duel* (1971).

Childhood under the Eye of the Secret Police: the original subtitle (the paperback was to say simply, *A Memoir*) felt the oppressive weight of *under* as well as that of another sensing, another medium: under the *Ear* of the Secret Police, too. Some of the most degrading moments in *Burying the Typewriter* and in the poems uncoil from what the secret police hear (and say), thanks to their microphones; what they record and transcribe; then succeeded by a further uncoiling of what Bugan herself now has come to hear and to say, to record and to transcribe— better, to translate from Romanian to English and to transpose it all from the grey inhumanity of the documents to the deep colours of her art. 'Legends' has on facing pages —on confronting pages—both the secret police document [Strictly Secret / Exemplary Unique/ Transcribed P.A.] and her own helpless remonstration that its record simply has to be false ('He could not have known that code-name'):

> Your words, P.A., are in my father's mouth
>
> and today it seems I read a version of ourselves
> narrated in your own language that makes it
>
> plain to see how you recorded and transcribed
> our fears, how we lived without a choice.

Writing in English, Bugan is yet vigilant to honour her responsibilities to her own native language. The Appendix to *Releasing the Porcelain Birds*, after the body of the book has presented the secret police transcripts that she has made into an art of truth, reproduces 'excerpts from the original copies of secret police surveillance files in Romanian', the aim being 'to give a visual sense of the historical material that led to the making of these poems, and a sense of the original secret police language for those who can read Romanian'. She honours, too, her other responsibilities:

I thank the Center for the Study of the Archives of the Securitate (CNSAS) for giving me access to the archives of surveillance documents on my family and for reassuring me that I can publish these documents. I also thank my family for allowing me to publish the excerpts from our archive that appear in the current book in my literal translation. The language of the translations reflects the secret police-speak in the original files: I made no effort to correct the grammar or improve the flow of the transcripts.

Reassuring me! Drily punctilious, so straight the face that leaves it at that. (For now, or anyway for here.) 'Correct the grammar or improve the flow': one cadence that might just be audible is the fall of a tyrant. His fall was destined to a firing squad.

> His fall was destined to a barren strand,
> A petty fortress, and a dubious hand;
> He left the name at which the world grew pale
> To point a moral or adorn a tale.
>
> Johnson, *The Vanity of Human Wishes*

Words, with their own lives and deaths, can be devoted ('Defaced, deflowered, and now to death devote') to apprehending the containment of *dead ground*. The figure of speech might mean—might proffer—something to someone arriving at a new terrain, as Beckett did with French, and Bugan with English. These particular francophones and anglophones may possess a benign counterpart—and counter-resistance—to those microphones of malignity. We may speculate (while needing, as well, a verb that is based etymologically not on the eye of flesh but on the ear) about the ways of words that cross to other words—words that may be out of sight but are not necessarily out of mind; out of eyeshot but not always out of earshot; alive within what may prove to be dead ground. Words, though few, had succeeded in crossing from the rooms of the family home in Romania to a location that is not exactly a room at all: a cell.

> We hung onto those few words that could cross
> The clay-like murky territories between us.
>
> > 'A birthday letter'

Could cross because no one would ever double-cross? And *territories* not only because of earth's clay, and disinterring, but because such a secure word can put up some resistance to the prospect of terror?

The reader, this reader, may be imagining these intimations of a cellarage. True, and a warning may be in order. 'The jailer warned him not to talk about what had happened there.' Understood. But then exactly how much are we to understand, to gather, at a related moment of 'A birthday letter'?

> Each word was limitless,
>
> > clothed our souls and warmed against despair,
> > shielded us from their world of terror

—*warmed* against? That, solely?

> I see us in our small kitchen that first night standing
> > around each other
> Not knowing what to say
>
> > > 'Found in secret police records'

—but careful *not* to say 'standing *by* each other', for she knows that this is not for her to say (even while she does well to intimate the thought, and we know what she means). And there is the close of the opening poem, 'We are museums':

even the illusion that
There might have been *something* we could have kept for ourselves.

—how touchingly this keeps to itself the force of that other preposition: 'could have kept to ourselves'. Art's power is that it both does and does not keep things to itself. In this it conducts itself like a responsible family. ' "Butnaru" at the visit with his daughter':

> I said that life is hard
> no wood for winter, no one to help,
> school year finished well, and I aim to go to University

—*aim to*, not *am* to, for that would be counting chickens.

> I sat in silence weighting apples, pears and plums
> against mesmerizing gallops across distant prairies.

'There'

—meanwhile *waiting* (without mentioning the matter), and weighing, to a scruple, the difference between what it is to weigh and what it is to weight.

Time to unearth the last of these speculations of mine: how should we weigh or weight the chances of Carmen Bugan's having turned, whether consciously or not, when she turned to English, to a reticent resource, something of a dead ground: her father's Christian name?

Ion.

Romanian has not only its form of the name John but the scientific noun. Yet English might be glimpsed—not overheard, for the pronunciation is other—as adding an extraordinary range of words, from *ion* (noun) in itself to *-ion* as an indispensable ubiquitous suffix. I risk presumption, but.

The name *Ion* stands out more than once in the secret police transcripts that are reproduced, some in English, some in Romanian. 'The aforementioned objects belong to escapees Bugan Ion and P.T'—one such obj. being '(one) English-Romanian dictionary'. 'The inmate Bugan Ion has to execute 3746 days of incarceration'. The poem in pain, '3746 days', confronting the transcript, simply addresses her father as you. (But in the knowledge, and perhaps intimating, that Ion's pronunciation in Romanian is, roughly, *you-on*.) Granted, she could very well have found herself translating into her English the Romanian word for 'incarceration' without ever catching sight of Ion … incarceration. (Or of *aforementioned … Ion … dictionary*.) But she does write of herself as 'daughter / of convict with a code-name' (and with code-names in his world: 'He could not have known that code-name'). The honourable coding of a Christian name within a poem might incarnate discretion as well as valour. And other impulses: at news of the amnesty, 'In his prison cell my father's jubilation was recorded'. Whereas *Ion… incarceration* has a negative charge, *father's jubilation* is positively charged.

ion: Electr. 'Any individual atom, molecule, or group having a net electric charge (either positive or negative).' Inmate Bugan Ion ('3746 days'):

> signing his own sentence by which atoms
> of his own blood, particles smaller still
>
> will be born from the combustion of his mind
> racing beyond the speed of light:

—a sentence that is signed (in its way), born again from the combustion of her mind, with *Ion* born from *combustion*, a sequence itself born from the transcript's *Ion … incarceration*.

Or there are sinister coincidences of the *ion trap*: 'a device designed to catch ions; *spec.* one in a cathode-ray tube or television camera that prevents ionized molecules from reaching the screen or the target'. ('device': OED *surveillance*: attrib. esp. of devices, vessels, etc., used in military or police surveillance. The Bugan home: 'the room equipped

with listening devices'. 'target': 'We have become / "objects of observation," "targets" '.)

> Arm in arm in the old quarters searching for his hotel
> where he hid from police, the trap door that is
> no longer there.

'Any angle of a fortification, the ground before which is unseen': but
surveillance had seen to it that 'There are no secrets anyway'. Except, it
may be, those of art and its memorializing.

> For words, like Nature, half reveal
> And half conceal the Soul within.

Ars est celare—not only as transitive verb, and concealing not *artem*
alone …

Andrew Kahn

The Return

Да я лежу в земле,
Губами шевеля…

Here I lie in the earth,
Moving my lips…

THE RUSSIAN HAMLET of Cherdyn' is on nobody's bucket-list. It is about 1500 km east of Moscow as the crow-flies. The problem is that the crow does not fly in that part of the world (nor do jailbirds). 'You are going into the Zone,' said Russian friends in Oxford. By which they did not exactly mean the film-maker Andrei Tarkovsky's metaphysical space, though not exactly not it either. The Zone signifies the vast territory on which the camps of the Gulag were situated and where prisoners or zeks often settled after their release, an area of marginality and criminality. Cherdyn' was the first location in the sentence of exile for the great poet Osip Mandelstam and his wife Nadezhda in 1934. Under armed guard they made the arduous journey by train and boat. When the reality of isolation and memory of interrogation sank in, Mandelstam briefly lost his mind on arrival and jumped out of the window of a hospital. Their appeal to an old friend, the Bolshevik Bukharin, got them transferred to Voronezh, much closer to the Russian heartland. Later, when Mandelstam's sanity was restored, he wrote a small set of poems about the journey by river. In one of them he imagines having the power to shape-shift and swim off; in another, he wonders whether he might, like Chapaev, the hero of the enormously popular 1920s film about a revolutionary hero, swim across the river to his escape (he knew full well that Chapaev didn't make it).

A group of fellow lovers of Mandelstam, mainly Muscovites, roped me in to making the trip seventy-five years later virtually to the day. Outside Perm, land and water seemed to change places. Roads wove in and out alongside the vast Siberian tributaries undulating through the terrain, the streams and rivers sometimes as wide as lakes, in the shallows dotted with the solitary angler after bream or carp. Nikolai Pobyl', one of our Muscovite friends, praised the fly-fishing, even better, he said, further north. Further north seemed unattainable and frightening. You looked out the window to flat landscapes and no road signs; you looked up through the window to endless sky, and then down to endless sky reflected in the broad rivers and streams.

The school bus rolled out of Perm in late evening. Our band acquired somewhere along the way a female minder with the leather-jacket and dark glasses that were her firm's trademarks. She whipped out notepad or tape-recorder sparingly ('Could you speak into the microphone slowly?', she asked me, 'and tell me your name?'). At ten o'clock at night the sun was vertical. The road was riven with fissures, the bus nearly poleaxed by palatial potholes. You who enter here leave behind any hope of shock-absorbers. Around 2 a.m. we halted adjacent to a church complex glowing by the side of the road. In the steely moonlight the white outer wall gleamed like a sheet of aluminium, the onion dome had a dark sheen. At eye level everything was pitch black, an effect of uncanny chiaroscuro. This was the beautiful Solikamsk Trinity Monastery, closed off by a green metal gate and rusty padlock. Built in the sixteenth century, from 1928 it had been used as a transit point into the Gulag system. An icon above the gate looked freshly restored. It might have been a copy of the famous Rublev Trinity. On the wall dully shone a bronze plaque dedicated to the writer Varlaam Shalamov. Everyone knows Solzhenitsyn, but Shalamov is the Turgenev of the camps, the most lyrical and brutal of prose poets. The inscription's letters are in the chunky style of a woodcut; the upper half as a bas-relief representing stick-figures, the small people of Russian history, with Shalamov (later a friend of Nadezhda Mandelstam) in profile. This was the start of his life as a *zek* in Kolyma, the harshest network of camps in the Zone. Hours later we arrived at the town and travelled by van down to the river—the bus was no match for the muddy tracks. Mandelstam's meaning in the poem 'The day stood at five heads' felt immediate and personal. Distance seemed to have added another quartile to the clock.

Cherdyn' lies along a tributary of the Kama River. Here its stream is sluggish and like a lagoon. Our guest house, built in the Finnish style, was riverside. Some of our fellow travellers had digs closer to town. These included Olga, an engineer by profession and by love the secretary of the Mandelstam Society, who shared a room with our snitch. Our guest house came with its own enigma. The sex of the caretaker was unclear—by sight and sound a woman who used masculine verb endings. We bunked two to a room in the comfortable lodge. Meals were taken at a long table with plenty of drink in the Russian style. Untied tongues talk poetry or recite. Nikolai, a short white-haired man with a stubby nose and splendid forelock, nightly presided and took requests. 'Name a poet, name a poem!' His body would begin to sway, he'd rock on the balls of his feet just a little and dance slightly. His body vibrated, he hummed as though his entire body were a tuning fork, and then the recital began. All poets, any lines, any quantity of lines flowed out of him by the dozen, by the hundreds. He was a miracle of poetic memory and adoration.

The town of Cherdyn' is built on the hillock above the river. Unemployment among the local youth is apparently in the 40% range; they looked as friendly as the numerous stray dogs. One main street contains brick municipal offices from the late imperial period, including the hospital, the site of Mandelstam's trauma in June of 1934. There is a main area—not quite a square since covered in planks and mud—featuring a small market and truckers' café. Side streets peter out quickly, merging into birch groves. A gaudy Lenin—made of a gleaming silver material of a kind that lines chewing-gum wrappers—stands outside the municipal buildings. Two eighteenth-century churches of Italianate design lend height and an unexpected trace of European Russia. From one campanile the sky seemed to curve slightly.

Our business was to commemorate Mandelstam. A plaque was unveiled on the outer wall of the hospital where he tried to kill himself. This rectangle, made appropriately of slate, a Mandelstamian stone, carries a handsome image of the poet from the 1920s, reproduces lines from his poem 'The Age' and these simple words of commemoration: 'The poet Osip Mandelstam, subjected to repression, lodged in this building in 1934.' Cherdyn' became base camp for coach excursions further north into the so-called Five Small Towns, tiny villages settled in the seventeenth century. In the seventeenth century, these were places of exile for the odd deposed royal (we were shown the pit and chains), as well as havens for prospectors heading for Siberia. Before 1917, this region provided most Russian salt, transported down the Kama, its mining rights owned by the Stroganov family. Their local wealth financed a once splendid estate on the banks of the Kama foregrounded by a shanty town of shacks plopped down in some wetlands. The extant eighteenth-century buildings are now under restoration as a cultural centre. A wing of the splendid mansion was light and airy; a parterre and terrace descended from the back of the house onto the river. There were no barges or barge-haulers but we were joined by a quixotic young poet who earns a living impersonating as a *skomorokh*, a medieval itinerant jester, performing for children and visitors.

The eighteenth-century interiors of the palace had been stripped out, probably looted during the Civil War period. The modern lunch room was smart and clean and the food something of a pick-me-up. Scarcely anyone noticed the silent old man (I only ever caught the first initial of his name and then later in the day) who joined our party, most likely in order to hitch a ride, a necessity for people who live along the river. Buses have their own zones of sociability. R. sat at the very back, its own Pale of Settlement. Olga, a real chatterbox of excellent Russian, resumed her place at the front but had become broody. Her room-mate, the security stooge, was in the adjacent seat across the aisle. Olga turned to her and exploded in taunts (the word 'louse' in Russian is *gnida* and that very long 'e' sound was like a needle). Nobody moved away, nobody spoke, and when the torrent of sarcasm had run its course Olga's victim withdrew to the back of the bus, a second passenger in the rear alongside the stony old man.

We packed up next morning. The announced itinerary on the way back to Perm involved some sightseeing and local stops, that was all, before the train journey back to Moscow at 3 a.m. In the early afternoon, and now in the home stretch, we pulled off the road onto a lane. This stop was by popular demand. Someone had spotted a birch forest and an emerald glint. 'Moss!' The moss that grows in this tundra is a springy cushion, suspended not above the abyss but on spongy bog. So we had all piled off and fanned out into the forest treading gently on a wondrous bed of shimmering green. About an hour later we pulled off for another stop. This time nothing had caught anyone's eye. Pavel, our geographer friend, scholar of genocide, and worshipper of Mandelstam, herded us off. We shuffled a few hundred yards down a neglected lane on one side bordered by a wooden fence. Pylons and barbed-wire ran along on the other side. The road led to a kiosk and we waited for Pavel's instructions.

We were stood in front of Perm-36, a labour camp in the Soviet penal archipelago. In 1946 Perm-36 was created for political prisoners and prisoners of conscience. It closed in 1987, and in 1994 the Museum of the History of Political Repression was opened (and remains open despite its loss of funding, the precariousness of its existence recognized in the Watch List of Endangered Sites maintained by the World Monuments Fund). This is the only extant camp from the GULAG system. Inside the gate an inner precinct is marked out by a whitewashed wall, much like the masonry surrounding the Solikamsk Monastery or any medieval Russian historic town. Watchtowers, some atop buildings, some freestanding, dot the perimeter. A gap of about fifty yards separates an inner wooden fence and the outer wooden fence. The air was milky and dull, burdock everywhere a sign of neglect. The fence resembled the driftwood from which the shantytown was made. Weathered and grey, about six feet high, its scale is not imposing. Nothing like the overt and hellish mockery of the gate at Auschwitz glares out at you. Mere splinters, it seems, can pen people in. Nature provided much empty sky and empty terrain to help keep them there. The amount of unused space inside the camp is surprising—openness is not a friend. Buildings are low and single storey. There is a log cabin, made by prisoners, with a pitched roof, identified as a place of solitary confinement when jail cells did not work. Dormitories are stark and basic, and beds either in rows, sometimes separated by a screen, or tiered for prisoners to bunk up.

Olga had become frantic with anxiety; the rest of us proceeded into the exhibition space spread out over several rooms. The interior was much like the ethnographic and regional museums you find everywhere in provincial Russia: the glass and pine cases, labels written out in hand or typed in now faded ink, and lining paper were all standard Soviet issue. On display were the primitive tools prisoners used for their forced labour. They looked like artefacts from a museum of the Stone Age. Unusually, and a reminder that this a place of incarceration was now a site of education, the cases contained legal dossiers of individual *zeks*: prison photos, charge sheets, court room transcripts, and judicial sentences stamped and signed. The presence of legal documentation reflected the involvement of the Moscow-based group Memorial whose brave efforts to archive every aspect of the Gulag and to preserve eyewitness testimony continues to face huge resistance. From somewhere ahead—we shuffled along slowly and the tail lost the head of the group—there was a commotion. People huddled in only to find R. standing silently in front of a glass case at shoulder height. Olga excitedly pointed to a photograph and the paperwork of a prisoner from the early 1970s and asked him, 'It's you, isn't it? It's you!' Everyone stared, comparing photo and original and the resemblance was undeniable. Like Shalamov, the old man had gone stone deaf in the camp. He nodded to confirm that it was him, and very quietly told us that he was an artist whose paintings had been non-conformist. So jailbirds did fly, after all. In fact, a sketch of one work of 'decadent' art was displayed there. R. had never been back to Perm-36 after serving his sentence. Resigned and dignified, he resumed his place in the back of the coach and then quietly and just as he had joined us, without either greeting or farewell, he asked the driver to leave him by the side of the road before we reached the city.

Understatement marked Perm-36—or, in fact, no statement. A painful silence spoke of a horror of neglect more sinister than coercion. The lowest definition of utility and subsistence determine living space. Rooms were not prison cells but the only distinguishing feature that differentiated them was the fact that one set of rooms had an open frame (leading nowhere), the other bars (leading nowhere). Space had no extension here—the distance from A to B was the same as never moving from A. Why have cells at all? And perhaps pointlessness was the point—that there was always one degree more of deprivation left. The Russian word *zabroshennost'* came to mind: it means neglect to the point of decay and denigration. Everywhere sound was muffled, deadened as though there was no sound to the sound. Was this the voice of 'indifferent nature' that Pushkin said grew around the grave? But Pushkin also wrote about the music of exile that had stayed with him as a plenitude. For him that was the sea. This was the music of absence or the absence of music, a vacuum. Auschwitz was a killing field. The horror of this place was a pervasive sense of life as decay, an insidious and life-sapping inertia accompanied by noiselessness. We had been in the Zone but not of it. R. had been of it, and returned full of that silence and nature's deafness, and then slipped away.

Leo Mellor

Forbidden Landscapes

SOMETIMES A COUNTRY ROAD takes a ninety-degree turn, and the tarmac abruptly changes direction. The original way, straight ahead, was decisively blocked off a while ago. The concrete blocks still echeloned across the way are not necessarily visible; their bulk is lost in brambles which then tangle into a shaggily unflailed hedge. Something prickles on the back of the neck, a sense of curiosity rises, even as you continue on the realigned route. What lies beyond that ditch, the lazily looped razor-wire, and those hazel thickets?

Even the knowledge that what lies beyond is a military training area does not dispel the mystery. Standing at the perimeter natural inquisitiveness is hard to contain, or even confine to the actually observable: each innocuous smudge on the horizon looks like it could be meaningful, and amid the cracking of far off rifle fire is the sense of soldiers getting down to 'serious-play'. For what might it be like to pretend— as realistically as possible—to fight and kill? What kind of terrain is needed to enable this?

Across Britain the Ministry of Defence remains one of the great land-owners, holding a vast acreage for different uses. Its training areas— clustered on Salisbury Plain, moors in the Northumbria and Cumbria, and in south Wales—share common factors: they are all forbidden landscapes to most civilians most of the time, and their usefulness comes from artifice—and the scale of space they take up. For they have to be big enough for overshoots and live-firing, for deployment and assessment; but they also have to contain enough *stuff*—from Soviet-era radars to mock villages—to make the sheer slog of manoeuvring soldiers on the ground realistic enough to be useful.

Within the training areas the exercises that are devised to train soldiers come complete with plot-twists and narrative arcs, and utilise the different kinds of topography in different ways. They are thus not just rehearsals for the 'theatres of war' but places inherently concerned themselves with different kinds of performance. The actual pre-history of these areas bears no relationship—apparently—to how they are now used. Yet such 'serious play' unlocks the paradoxical nature of these landscapes: they are meant to be stage sets, zones cleared of inhabitants and thus available for any scenario; however, in fact, they are places where both the past and the future can be strangely glimpsed.

Looking at the inland Breckland sand-dunes of East Anglia, in 1677, the diarist John Evelyn observed: 'The Travelling Sands … that have so damaged the country, rolling from place to place, like the Sands in the Deserts of Lybia, quite overwhelmed some gentleman's whole estates.'

The history of this part of England is one of chronic instability: from rivers diverted by powdery drifts to questions that go camouflaged as jokes: 'is your farm in Suffolk or Norfolk?' Answer: 'it depends which way the wind is blowing'. Indeed Robert Macfarlane once called the Brecklands 'England's Arabia', noting how this local sand (and sand-storms and sand-dunes) created not just a version of the Empty Quarter near Norwich, but also prepared the British Army for its wars which were fought many miles further south or east. The military training area in the Brecklands, STANTA, is a space I have circled around, following the contours of its edges, not joining the waiting list for once-a-year carefully shepherded tours.

But even on the civilian side of the perimeter fence some of the make-believe leaks out into the wider area. The sandy tracks look innocuous and Thetford Forest has plenty of neatly waymarked paths and a Center Parc dome. Yet, despite huge efforts in planting trees since the 1920s, this landscape still seems to be shifting and unsettled, even when the sand is obscured: shallow lakes called pingos ponds wax and wane in a sequence nobody fully understands, and though the smell of pine trees could calm, you soon realise that they are planted in remorseless geometrical grids and every track is also a booby-trapped visual trick of depth-perception.

Since 1942, on this scrubby-plain north-east of Thetford, the British Army has practised for war. The bucolic names of ghost villages evacuated in the Second World War now refer mainly to stumps of masonry and the odd preserved church—a litany of West Tofts, Buckenham Tofts, Sturston, Langford, Stanford, and Tottington. Here also lies a micro-history of different manoeuvres inscribed into the land through explosions; traces of doctrinal changes in military tactics (should infantry accompany tanks? Clear villages without air-support?). But they also mean nobody wanders blithely through the gigantic sheep pastures (with approximately fifteen sheep lost a year to bullets or explosions) or sprays organophosphates: the naturalist Richard Mabey still calls the roadless and housing-free plain, with no tillage or fences, 'the closest we can get to walking in a Neolithic landscape'.

But at the edges there are structures, in 2008 the MoD spent £14million building a replica Afghan village at Bridge Carr. This was the latest successor to a lineage of other ersatz hamlets and mock settlements across Britain—with their mix of carefully smudged realism covering their theatrical backways and changeable scenery. Since the 1950s they have been spaced out, originally using the actual buildings of the villages that were requisitioned, and designed so soldiers can practice their FIBUA skills (Fighting in Built Up Areas). Yet even the best current simulacrum in the make-believe village of 'Shardlik', with ex-Gurkhas playing parts, and a 'scent-system' wafting out smells of rotten meat and sewage, could not fully capture what the unofficial military acronym FISH & CHIPS (Fighting In Someone's Home & Creating Havoc In Peoples Streets) more accurately denotes. Indeed Shardlik is now becoming a ruin too, joining the versions of East German collective farms and Northern Irish hamlets which, after their usefulness had expired, were as emphemeral as expired stage-sets—and probably burnt or bulldozed. But in some places new drifts of sand—formed as the ground cover is torn up by tracked vehicles—has begun to cover their remains, creating a gnomic archaeological layer for future generations.

At the other end of England is RAF Spadeadam in Cumbria, 9600 acres of moor and blanket-bog. It is mainly used for what the RAF term 'operationally-representative electronic warfare training', so this is where the scenarios played out on the ground are interpreted—or fought—by pilots from the air. Spadeadam is filled with ways of baffling both systems and humans; there are the sensors for illuminating the aircraft as they follow the hillside contours, and jammers for distracting their weapons. The US Airforce still terms their missions to find and destroy radars as 'Wild Weasel' operations, and while the RAF does not have such jaunty slang their need to practice SAM (Surface to Air Missile) suppression, while gaining plausible techniques for evasion, means fighter-bombers ply back and forth daily through an interlocking set of arcs and meshes of fine-pulsed signals.

Below these reverberations in the air, the whole site at Spadeadam fascinates. Thickly strewn with immoveable and mute structures, the land hides disused missile silos under the blanket of Sitka Spruce plantations, along with an extraordinary ferro-concrete set-piece: a line of three twenty-five-metre-tall gantries jutting out over a valley. Placed near the centre of the site, and therefore now rarely seen by anyone other than those who practise for war in its shadow, this is a masterwork which could rival St Peter's Seminary at Cardross, the brutalist debt to Le Corbusier which still in its gaunt disuse hangs over the Clyde; or even the gigantic Sound Mirrors, those 1920s precursors of radar, which are still reflecting whatever they can pick-up from the shingle at Dungeness.

Spadeadam's history is bound-up with post-war British rocketry; it was created as a place suitable remote from habitation to experiment with intermediate range missiles—especially Blue Streak with its dangerously unstable fuel. But these gaunt concrete test-stands, now fenced off and slowly corroding, were built in the 1950s to be the proving-rigs for Britain's abortive space programme. The stands allowed rocket engines to be run full-thrust while remaining tethered: they are mute testimony to a mix of prescient techno-futurism (our current world of satellites and GPS) and now-defunct post-war military technology. The gantries remain sullen structures, with splayed angles and great legs rooted in deflector dishes, and yet their real pathos is in their testimony to a future which never happened. The rocket tested here called Black Knight was cancelled in 1971 after only one successful launch from Woomera in Australia; the satellite that it finally lobbed aloft was called Prospero—and this still continues to circle the earth in a stable orbit, a techno-shard of a future that never happened. The naming was surely not accidental: Prospero in the *Tempest* renounced his powers; and Britain is the only country in the world to have started and given up a space programme.

Traces of a ghost future is however only part of a story, for what Spadeadam is famous for now, among people of certain industries, is not aerial potential—but infernos and crumpled metal. For in another part of the wood, or rather in a cleared valley, there is an elongated soot-marked concrete pad thick with apparatus: and here another kind of testing still takes place. Since the 1970s, a commercial company has been running large-scale fire, explosion and blast testing here, simulating gas pipe ruptures or 'catastrophic failures'. Their short films make clear that while Spadeadam is 'tailored to meet specific customer requirements and support a unique range of test scenarios' it is also a wild place which can act as a neutral backdrop for simulated disasters. Such constructed destruction tests not only the resilience of structures already built out in the real world but also those currently being designed for future resource exploitation: here, prototype oil-rig parts will be blown up, before the rig is even constructed.

Cycling through rain and rain again, my memories are of a single track-road rising out of one valley and dropping to the next, then blocked tracks and a minimal guardhouse under a bruised grey-black sky. Up on Mynydd Epynt north of Brecon a vast plateau was taken over by the War Office in 1940. It remains in military hands, 31,000 acres suitable for endurance training and live-firing. Those who fought in the Falklands favourably compared the march across the mountains to Port Stanley with Mynnydd Epynt's sodden expanses and rocky outcrops, a landscape of peat bogs and channels, with deep-cut valleys of rivers draining south.

Over seventy years of military control has also reshaped the landscape: there are now turning circles and great waiting areas: each de-embarkation point is a stage for hurry-up-and-waiting. Other patterns can only be seen from the air; gashes and scars, especially where wild fires burn after training, mottle the flanks of the hills.

The clearances of Mynydd Epynt in 1940, with 219 people having to leave their farms, can be understood as part of what a wartime state simply did (or had to do) in the most terrifying days of expected imminent invasion. The good of the whole—and the defeat of Nazism—justified much, and the exceptionalism of wartime led to apparent mass acceptance.

The melancholia of the pictures taken during the evictions, especially those by Iorwerth Peate from March 1940, has led to mourning a moment of cataclysmic shift—a day when everything changed. But everything has kept on changing since—due to who (and where) the British State was fighting and who could be employed to maintain the sprawling site. When interviewed in the 1980s a farmer gestured to the ranges and said 'I live over there, beyond East Germany…' Crossing the plateau is the 'Burma road', constructed by Italians and German PoWs, memorialising another track in a different war.

Patrick Wright, in his book *The Village that Died for England*, tracked the history of Tyneham in Dorset after it was taken over by the military; but he also traced how *because* it was frozen in time Tyneham became a redolent symbol for people to project versions of nationhood, of Deep England untouched by immigration or an organic rural community. Yet there is something in the very act of the military appropriating the land at Mynydd Epynt in 1940 that can be felt to be part of a longer colonising continuum, another marker of English attitudes towards Welsh-speaking rural Wales, and the people who lived there.

The presumption that the local Welsh were peasants without agency, or at any rate impediments to progress, also justified other diktats from government. In the twentieth-century the rise of Welsh Nationalism can be correlated against such decisions, from the siting of a bombing range on the Llŷn peninsula in the 1930s—which provoked a symbolic and celebrated arson attack by Lewis Valentine, D. J. Williams and Saunders Lewis, memorialised as 'Tân yn Llŷn' ('fire in Llŷn'); through to the drowning of Capel Celyn in the 1960s to create a reservoir to supply Liverpool with drinking water.

The physical landscape of Wales was seen as a resource for a unitary British state, but in doing so nurtured one of the forces which might yet pull the state asunder. The cultural expression of why a landscape might matter, and how it might resist appropriation, comes in many different forms. A few years before his death the poet and artist David Jones composed 'The Sleeping Lord'. Shorter than his book length works *The Anathemata* or *In Parenthesis*, it similarly wove Arthurian mythology with actual topography—yet now he was not roaming across European history or the WWI battlefields of Flanders. Rather the poem arced back to Jones' time in Capel-y-ffin, a few miles east of the Epynt, where he stayed in 1925. Jones creates in the poem a lament for the use and misuse of Welsh land—but also an animating spirit within the hills themselves; this is thus a work of mourning and potential, especially in the final lines which wonder:

> Is the configuration of the land
>   the furrowed body of the lord
> are the scarred ridges
>   his dented greaves
> do the trickling gullies
>   yet drain his hog-wounds?
> Does the land wait the sleeping lord
>   or is the wasted land
> that very lord who sleeps?

What other versions of a secular uncanny, of something inexplicable and yet compelling, are still hidden in these near-impossible to reach places? My fascination is only partly driven by their strange histories, their mix of destruction plus preservation (or even, as MoD press officers would have it, preservation *because of* destruction). I like the way they are alien because they remain both wild and tamed, but also because they have produced a kind of image debris, cropping up in the corners of the cultural imagination when least expected.

A year ago I felt a flinch of recognition as I flipped through CDs in a charity shop. One album's cover image was still unsettling and unforgettable: it portrayed a carcass of a military aircraft, grounded at an odd angle on moorland, its fuselage scabbed by small-arms fire. In the background there was just the green-grey hills and the lowering sky. It was *Sci-fi Lullabies*, a compilation of B-sides by the British band Suede, an album I had listened to on its release in 1997. The cover photograph was taken at the Otterburn Ranges, a vast tract of Northumbrian moorland given over to live firing with all calibre of weapons, from rifles to tanks. Suede's forlorn aircraft—polished by gunfire to metamorphosis—is melancholic; but juxtaposed with the album's title something else emerges. For these places dedicated to military training might seem to offer a kind of pre-enactment for imagining wars elsewhere. Perhaps these terrains, in their mix of secrecy and violence, give hints of what a post-climate crisis future might look like—and it is both frightening and captivating. Thus training areas might actually be training us, firstly in how to unlock the hidden past from debris and stories, but also through suggesting how the future, and whatever lullabies might remain in times to come, could be imagined or sung.

Paul Hodgson

Slippage *and* Train

IN THE SUMMER of 1914, as diplomatic efforts to prevent a world war lost ground, troops were mobilized in preparation for conflict. The military campaigns that followed over the next four years were unlike any that had preceded them. The nature of combat was changed irreversibly, with huge numbers of soldiers, armaments and supplies being mobilized with speed and precision, through the use of railways and Standard time. Technological advancements in artillery and rapid-fire weaponry lead to an unprecedented loss of life. The effects of mechanized warfare forced a monumental shift in human consciousness to take place, creating a decisive rupture between a time before and a time after the events of the war.

Slippage is one of a series of works that I made for inclusion in an exhibition commemorating the 90th anniversary of the Battle of the Somme. The focus of this work is an image of a fallen horse; an incident that creates spectacle, and provides a visual jolt within a carefully constructed studio set. The photographic nature of the image encourages us to place this key event in a temporal sequence, leading us to imagine the moments just before the horse collapsed, and to think about the changes that occurred immediately prior to the image being captured.

Train features two images of a horse-drawn cart placed one behind the other, in what could be the beginning of a longer line of mechanically driven units. Read from left to right, the work suggests a development of sorts, through changes in visual language. Both carts carry empty artillery cases, metal ware and saddles. In the second cart these items have been transformed through hand drawn elements, reminiscent of the type of pictorial language developed by artists during the early twentieth century, as they sought to better express their experience of a fast changing world.

The two images that follow are details chosen from the large-scale works described above.

James Macdonald Lockhart

Live Ground

FOR SEVERAL MONTHS now I've kept a thin, faded pamphlet on hold for me at the library. There's little chance of someone else wanting to borrow it. In fact, I wouldn't be surprised if I'm the only person to have requested it up from the vaults of the Bodleian library. Published in 1981, its full title is *The Royal Artillery Range Hebrides Natural History Society Benbecula—A Guide to Birds and Birdwatching on the Uists.* Only twenty pages of double-sided A4, stapled in the top left corner, the print fading in bands across the page. The type on some of the species entries is so faded it's hard to make out, as if the text has diminished to reflect the bird's rarity: 'Grey Phalarope, *Phalaropus fulicarius:* One seen on North Uist on 19 Sep 79 and two on South Uist on 2 Oct 79' / 'Mistle Thrush, *Turdus viscivorus:* One recorded on South Uist on 18 November 1979…'

A Guide to Birds and Birdwatching on the Uists has become a sort of dream book for me. I arrive at the library, request the brown card envelope the pamphlet fits inside, find a desk and dream up the birds, the bays and lochs the paper so methodically describes: 'April makes a great change in the bird life in the Uists. The geese, swans and thrushes leave for their northern breeding areas, and the Lapwings, Redshanks, Snipe and Ringed Plovers nest in profusion in the meadows…' / 'Pairs of Mute Swan breed on many scattered fresh water lochs, but the large non breeding population spends most of its time on Loch Bee…' On it goes like this, 150 species entries, from Black-throated Diver 'most likely to be found on the larger and remoter inland lochs on North Uist and Benbecula during the breeding season' to Manx Shearwater 'large numbers can be seen offshore, especially from Banranald, Grimnish

Point and in the Sound of Harris.' I am transfixed and transported. Sometimes, scrolling through the lists of birds, I find myself picking at an ink-scratch left by the typewriter as if it were a fleck of dirt. On the first page of the pamphlet, in the top right corner, there is an address and telephone number with a dated area code:

Royal Artillery Range Hebrides
BENBECULA
Scotland
PA88 5LN
Tel: Benbecula Military (0872-2384) Ext 208

I've wondered about trying that telephone number. It's long obsolete, of course. But I'm curious about it. Did anyone call Extension 208 when the number was in use? Was there a switchboard option? If you are calling about birds, press 1, for nuclear-armed guided missiles, it's 2...

I'm interested by the presence of the military in a paper about birds. I'd assumed the MOD would have little time for ornithology. Yet I learn from the pamphlet that the then secretary of the Royal Artillery Range Natural History Society was a 'Major D J R COUNSELL (Tel: Benbecula Ext 208)', that 'the MOD has a full time Conservation Officer who is responsible for the conservation of MOD land' and who is 'currently the Secretary of the Army Bird Watching Society'. I also learn that both the Army and Royal Air Force have ornithological societies which publish regular newsletters and journals. The Army's journal is called 'Adjutant' and subscription, in 1981, was £1 per year.

I like to read *A Guide to Birds and Birdwatching on the Uists* with my OS map of Benbecula & South Uist spread out over a neighbouring desk. Unfolding a map in the library is a tortuous process: rustle, crinkle... Shush! It sounds like I'm unwrapping tinfoil. Then I set the two—map and pamphlet—talking to one another. I note down potential viewing spots, circling them on the map: 'Stinky Bay & West Benbecula Lochs—These lochs hold wildfowl interest, whilst the surrounding terrain is recommended for general birding. Stinky (NF 760525) and Coot (NF 768510) Lochs are both highly recommended...'

So many lochs and lochans pattern the map of Benbecula & South Uist it looks as if the land is flaking. Aside from all this water, the other notable feature of the map is the long lines of bright red triangles demarcating several 'Danger Areas' along the west coast of South Uist. From Àird a Machair in the north following the coast for roughly 12 km south is all 'Danger Area', the red triangles marking out the perimeter of one of Europe's largest military air ranges. Many of the places the Uists bird guide describes coincide with these Danger Areas. At one point on the map, the OS symbol for a nature reserve—a small blue wading bird—wades in a loch which borders the Danger Zone.

In 1954 the UK government purchased the Corporal missile system—the world's first nuclear-armed guided missile—from the United States. Where to test such a missile with a range of eighty miles, away from urban populations, within the confines of the British Isles? The Outer Hebrides was one of the few places that met all the topographical requirements for a rocket range and, despite initial opposition and concern for the range's impact on the environment, archaeological sites and crofting townships, construction of the range on South Uist went ahead and has been in operation since the late 1950s. The range is located on the machair to the west of Loch Bì, a large freshwater loch which dominates the northern end of South Uist. There is a control centre and tracking station on Ruabhal, a hill just to the south of Loch Bì, which overlooks the range. And there is a further tracking station forty miles to the west on St Kilda. The main support centre for the range is at Balivanich on Benbecula from where army vehicles come and go along the road between the village and the range.

Over the last year I have made two visits to the Western Isles. In November I travelled to Benbecula and spent several days with its birds. There were snipe and lapwing in every field. At dusk, walking along the road south from Balivanich, huge flocks of starling whirled in black clouds above the farms. Greylag geese, wild and nervy, panicked into flight when I was still two fields away. The geese took off so heavily it looked as if they were dragging the field behind them. Walking along the shoreline I disturbed dozens of snipe from amongst piles of rusting kelp. Sometimes a snipe feeding through the wrack made me think the seaweed itself was quivering. I usually heard the snipe first, a snitch-snitch sound, like a speeded-up sneeze, then a flash of white breast as they burst away from under me. I was struck on that visit how the island's acoustics changed as I walked across it. I went, in the space of a mile, from this tremendous avian soundtrack—gulls, geese and waders in the west—to the silence of Benbecula's eastern moors. It was so quiet out on those hills I could hear a wren flicking through the dead bracken. And when a fieldfare flew across my path I could hear the sound the air made as it brushed the bird's wings.

I returned to the islands in July and this time spent most of my visit observing the birds on the missile range on South Uist. In November I'd kept my distance from the range, only aware of its presence through the radar domes perched on top of Ruabhal and the green army Land Rovers which often passed me on the road. I asked about the range in my B&B and learnt that it was an important local employer and currently operated by a private contractor on behalf of the MOD. I was also told that the range was often in use, with military forces from across NATO travelling to the Outer Hebrides to test missiles there. So I wasn't quite sure what to expect as I walked towards the first Danger Area marked on my map. Would I be able to enter? Would there be signs and flags warning me off?

But in the end there was nothing much, no flags, no sentries to block my way. Just a small sign with a map of the Danger Area, instructing the public to leave immediately when the red flags are hoisted or red beacon is lit. I walked in from the north, parking my car at the neat walled cemetery at Àird a Machair. There were oystercatchers and lapwings in amongst the graves, the oystercatchers calling in alarm as I passed. Two curlews came over, flying high then dropping down to circle above me. Flocks of starlings made shadows over the yellow flowers of the machair. There were skylarks and redshanks and ringed plovers. The redshanks peep-peep-peeping, fluttering up twenty feet,

a flash of white along the edge of their wings, circling in a noisy arc of agitation around their nest sites. A raven turned and croaked and a common tern went up from its nest to give the raven hell, twisting and jabbing at the huge black bird, harrying it away.

Walking across the missile range was a strange experience. I felt conspicuous. I was always in view of the range buildings and the tracking station with its complex of radar discs and domes on the hillside behind. The machair is such a vast open habitat, the sense of being watched as I walked though it never left me. I felt monitored, tracked. The presence of the base was unsettling. Perhaps I was silly to feel like this, nobody bothered me or told me to move on. Vehicles sped along the roads which linked the range's outbuildings but they never veered off towards me. Nevertheless I found it hard to shrug off that sense of being watched. I peered at the base through my binoculars, its radar discs cupped their giant ears back at me. I felt more relaxed when I dropped down through the dunes onto the beach. In the lee of the dunes I was out of view of the tracking station and observation towers on the range. Often I would sit with my back against the dunes watching the birds along the empty roar of the beach. Three ravens came tumbling through the wind. I watched an otter come out of the surf to feed on a white flatfish. No attempt to swallow the fish, just gnash-gnash-gnash, chewing off bits. Ringed plovers peeped then lifted into low fast flights across the sand. Black-headed gulls, in small groups, skimmed the top of the dunes. A whinchat with its creamy russet breast landed on a washed-up pallet a few feet from where I sat.

There is a tradition of giving names to rockets, or rocket parts, in order to diffuse the menace of the technology. It is a nomenclature defined by its incongruity. The trend being for the names to be as far removed as possible from the reality of the weaponry, so that they read like a code or secret language. The 'Christmas Tree Farm' for example is the name of the section on a Trident submarine which houses the nuclear missiles. A 'cookie cutter' is the term for a particular form of nuclear attack. A 'footprint', the pattern in which a nuclear bomb falls. Bird names too, just as incongruously, have been appropriated to soften the technology. The Corporal missile was replaced in the 1960s by the 'Skua' and 'Petrel' (with its 'Lapwing' motor) high altitude research rockets, both operated by the Atomic Weapons Research Establishment. There was also the 'Skylark' rocket with its 'Raven' motor and 'Goldfinch' booster, and a 'Fulmar' rocket, used in the late 70s, with its 'Heron' starting stage and a 'Snipe' upper stage.

That feeling of conspicuousness, of being watched whilst I was out on the missile range changed as I spent more time there. In one respect the feeling became more intense. But it shifted in its focus away from the military presence, away from the hardware, the radars and observation towers of the range, to the birds themselves. Ultimately, it was the birds monitoring my presence out there on the range, harassing me to move away from their nesting grounds. Sometimes that harassment was extremely uncomfortable. The most relentless of the birds were the common terns. Walking past their nest sites was to run a gauntlet. Suddenly a tern would come screaming towards me, making me flinch and duck as it dived low over my head, before turning sharply to make another pass. That long sharp bill, the tern's piercing yell… I just wanted to get out of the way as quickly as possible.

The slightest movement creates a ripple of awareness amongst the birds on the machair. When I am upright and walking amongst them, the oystercatchers and ringed plovers call repeatedly in agitation. But as soon as I sit down, make myself invisible, my back against a fence post, the birds are quiet. The oystercatchers relax, tuck their long orange beaks under their wings and doze. One or two birds stay alert and when I stand up and start to move, the sentries sound the alarm, jolting the other birds awake. The oystercatchers don't come as close as the terns, circling well beyond reach, cautious, their calls growing in tempo and pitch. One bird tries to draw me away by running along the ground away from its nest. A pause to check if I am following, then hurries on a little further, tugging me after it. Every bird in the vicinity knows I'm here. Every movement I make is clocked, monitored, assessed for threat.

By lifting birds such as snipe and lapwing off the machair and fitting their names into rocket parts, does that soften, does it placate, the technology? I think the gesture is too deliberate a distortion for that, an obfuscation of the reality. Perhaps the distortion is the point. If we did not gloss the rockets with something beautiful—a snipe, a goldfinch—we could not endure the reality of the rockets' capability. I'm not sure I could endure a world without birds. I know that their presence on the missile range in South Uist distorted the purpose of the range for me. The birds claimed the territory so loudly, so vigorously, so beautifully, the military presence, for me, shrunk beside them. And that's how it should be.

At the rifle-firing range there are bird droppings streaked down the numbers on the butts. Oystercatchers are perched on the fence posts along the rifle range as if marking the target distances off—50m, 100m, 250m… I stand in front of the butts watching the birds. Then, when I take a step towards them, it's as if I have triggered an alarm, every

oystercatcher takes off from its perch and the noise of their calling bounces off the butts. The oystercatchers even alert a small flock of starlings a hundred yards away. About a dozen starlings have arranged themselves in black dots over the sheet music of a wire fence. When I stand up, when the oystercatchers start up, the starlings detach from the wires before quickly settling back, rearranging themselves in a different score of notes along the fence.

Andrew McNeillie

In Memory of Private Roberts

Crossing the square in early spring,
Wreaths withered on the memorial,
Poppies bled by frost and snow,
I met Private Roberts reading
The roll call of the town's fallen.

'Armistice day? My pet aversion,'
Turning to me, his lip moist,
His thorny eye narrowed like a sniper's:
'Ior Evans? He'd never spent
A night away from home before,

Buried in Mad-a-gas-car.
Corner of a foreign field?
I doubt he'd ever heard of it.
Dai Sam? on Manchester
United's books in thirty-nine:

Buried in France. I bet
He's never remembered
At the going down of the sun
Or in the morning... Diw!
You know, I often contemplate

Siegfried Sassoon, chucking his medal away.
Never applied for mine.
All the way to Tobruk without
So much as a lance-jack's stripe,
I'm proud to say.

And Francis Ledwidge, born
The same day as Hedd Wyn,
And killed, you know, the same day
And in the same place too.
His comment: "To be called

A British soldier
While my country has
No place among nations..."'
He'd marched to Vesuvius
With Marcus Aurelius

In one breast-pocket and
The *Mabinogion* in the other,
An old campaigner
Over bog and heather
To find and fish the Serw stream:

Elusive, stubborn thread of water,
Of stygian glooms and mountain glances,
Its limpid, garrulous medium,
'Full,' as he said, 'of small trout
The length of a youth's hand.'

Nelson's Pillar, Dublin 1916

Nelson's Pillar decapitated 1966

Ian Ritchie

The Spire

O'CONNELL STREET is the heart of Dublin, and resonates with centuries of Irish history. Laid out in the 1740s as a grand, wide thoroughfare lined with terraces of handsomely proportioned buildings, it became a rich tapestry upon which the power struggle between the Irish people and their British colonial rulers found expression.

It provided the backdrop for uprisings and civil unrest, and was one of several prominent sites where monuments honouring British royalty and military leaders were erected in Dublin during the 18th and 19th centuries—tangible symbols of imperial power. Just as symbolically, these almost immediately became subject to vicissitudes ranging from insult and mutilation to relocation and destruction. A pantheon of Irish national heroes—from O'Connell and Parnell to the militant socialist Larkin—took their place and now only one remains: the non-figurative obelisk honouring the Duke of Wellington in Phoenix Park.

In the place of Nelson's Pillar, erected in O'Connell Street in honour of Nelson's victory at the Battle of Trafalgar in 1805 and blown up by the IRA in 1966, stands another non-figurative monument: the Spire of Dublin or Monument of Light (*An Túr Solais*).

Akin to standing stones—those most ancient, deliberate statements marking man's presence in the landscape—the obelisk and spire are shapes immunised against attack because they are not memorials, but history turned into markers; an invitation to passersby to search for the memorial in their own minds.

The Spire was designed to be a magnet, a place where there is nothing other than a notion of marking the centre, a space to be filled with the public's own hopes, aspirations and meanings. It is a monument to

Ireland's future rather than a commemoration of the past. Reaching out a reconciling hand to past and present, it embraces the various strands of Irish identity, dissolving the boundaries between Catholic and Protestant and taking into account Celtic traditions as well as those signifiers from Ireland's invaders.

The Spire of Dublin is for everyone to relate to, to be inspired by, perhaps to find their own centrality as it mirrors our images back onto ourselves.

The distinguished French domiciled Peruvian architect Henri Ciriani on the competition jury recognised it as a 'primary element, a freed point in the urban dynamic'.

The sociologist Professor Mary Corcoran, of the National University of Ireland, noted, 'The Spire of Dublin represents a vehicle for expressing a new kind of national and urban narrative, and for the economic revalorisation of the North side of the river.'

Frank McDonald, journalist and civic campaigner, wrote of it:

> This sensational structure will redefine the city centre
> and people's perceptions of where that is, quite apart
> from providing Dublin with a new icon. It addresses not
> only its immediate context in O'Connell Street, but also
> more distant views and even the city as a whole. One of
> Mr Ritchie's 'fundamental objectives' was to lift people's
> spirits, and it will certainly do that.

Even as the list of its witty nicknames grew, the Spire showed itself to be free of the dead hand of history—a monument which has escaped monumentality despite its height of four hundred feet. Mr Dick Gleeson, deputy chief planning officer of Dublin Corporation, said at the announcement of the winning design, 'It's understated, yet magnificently radical and powerful at the same time. Really, it's a work of art which will reinvent the public domain.'

Since the day its final segment was lifted into place in January 2003, to the sound of thousands cheering, its meaning has been appropriated by the public in wholly unexpected ways. By some it has been seen as a religious symbol pointing the way to heaven and God. It became a light sabre for the opening of a new Star Wars film and was lit green on St Patrick's Day, in collaboration with the UNESCO International Year of Light Ireland 2015. It became the screen for streaming a twitter feed displaying tweets with the dedicated hashtag #LightIRL—most appropriate for the Monument of Light.

IRELAND'S LIGHT

A monument inspired by the light
of Ireland's ever-changing skies
ever present by day and night.

Tall, elegant conical structure
symbolising growth, search, release,
thrust, optimism in Ireland's future.

Granite anchored underneath the street,
sliding past a bronze spiral base
a shell of peened silver stainless steel.

Urban line and point upon the site
softly reflecting sunlit clouds
while swaying in the wind, a night-light.

1998

© Ian Ritchie Architects photo Barry Mason

Tony Crowley

War and Art
The murals of Northern Ireland

IN THE EARLY seventeenth century, Sir Richard Fanshawe penned an ode 'Upon occasion of His Majesties Proclamation in the yeare 1630'. The point of the piece was to draw a distinction between the peace and harmony of Caroline Britain and the bellicose horrors inflicted across Europe by the Thirty Years War.

> Now warre is all the world about,
> And everywhere *Erynnis* raignes,
> Or else the Torch so late put out
> The stench remaines.

> Onely the Island which wee sowe,
> (A world without the world) so farre
> From present wounds, it cannot showe
> An ancient skarre.

The contrast was clear between Britain's 'White peace (the beautiful'st of things)', and the sectarian savagery ravaging Europe. And yet, of course, it isn't necessary to understand much of the history of the period to realise that retrospectively at least, Fanshawe's panegyric, is somewhat ironic, if not fantastical. Britain may well have withdrawn from its wars with Spain and France by 1630, but monarchical absolutism was in the process of engendering the brutalities of the English Civil War and the Confederate Wars in Ireland.

The opening of Fanshawe's poem is striking, though, and it has stuck with me since I first read it, particularly that resounding phrase 'warre is all the world about'. I have often thought of it while working in Northern Ireland, as I have, on a regular basis, since 1979, mostly taking photographs, though with a brief foray into journalism. War was indeed all the world about in Northern Ireland during most of that time, and the furies, reigned high and mighty in their various guises. And now that the conflict's torch has been extinguished, or at least temporarily dimmed, we are left, among other legacies, with the vile stench of the dirtiness of a war that lasted for almost thirty years (1969–1998).

As I have often been reminded when working in the North, I am fortunate in being able to leave, whenever I choose, to return to my job in a British university. Nevertheless, given the nature of the work in which I was engaged, I ran up against the realities of the war often enough. That didn't necessarily mean shootings or bombings, though I had more than my fill of that form of direct violence, but the ways in which war structures and conditions a society. Which is to say, the pervasiveness of war, its deep, seeping threat, the ways in which it got inside people's minds and bodies, its gradual emergence as a way of life.

Reflecting on that time now, I remember two dominant and recurrent experiences. A universal sense of expectant foreboding—the constant waiting for the next event: atrocity, mistake, spectacular, prison sentence, statement of political nonsense, banal tragedy. And semiotic paranoia—a state in which anything and everything (name, address, job, clothes, accent, school, sporting preference, newspaper, holiday destination…) was a sign and every sign was laden with political or conflict-related significance. They became reflexes: waiting in the dead ground and over-interpreting the things that only seem to be things.

My engagement with Northern Ireland, which became a life-long affair, began in 1979 when I spent my first summer vacation from Oxford University working as a student volunteer on a children's play-scheme in Divis Flats and the Lower Falls in West Belfast. As a working-class Liverpudlian, I had seen poverty and deprivation, but Divis was a different world entirely. It wasn't just impoverished, it was a war zone that featured regular, brutally violent conflict between the British Army and local Republican paramilitaries (the IRA and INLA). During my first year at the play-scheme, I became intrigued by the fact that in both Republican and Loyalist areas, public spaces—walls, pathways, advertising hoardings, street signs—were covered in social and political graffiti. Some of it was crude, some enigmatically coded, some humorous, and some politically sophisticated. Using a cheap camera, I began to record it; but just before I left in 1979, a Loyalist contact took me to photograph my first mural. Much of the symbolism was lost on me, but the mural featured an appeal to 'Remember the Loyalist prisoners' and a commemoration of the Queen's Silver Jubilee in 1977.

I was told at the time that muralism was a Loyalist practice which dated back to the inception of Northern Ireland in 1922 (murals had traditionally been painted in working-class areas to celebrate the 12th of July anniversary of the Battle of the Boyne). When I returned in 1980, however, I noticed a few Republican murals, mostly around the Beechmount area, in the mid Falls. A year later, there were many more Republican murals in Belfast and Londonderry/Derry (or stroke city as it's called by neutrals), most of which related to the 1981 Hunger Strike. The appearance of these murals marked the beginning of an astonishingly sustained artistic practice: it is calculated that between 1979–2017, something of the order of 25,000 murals have been painted in Northern Ireland.

Commissioned by paramilitary groups, political parties, local communities, and the State, they have ranged from simple depictions of violence, to sophisticated representations of history; from expressions of identity, to the articulation of international solidarity; from demands for political reform, to poignant appeals for peace. Once dismissed as mere propaganda, they are now recognised as a significant practice of public art and form one of the most popular attractions of Northern Ireland's burgeoning tourist industry. Once urban ephemera at best, agit-prop at worst, they are now commodified as 'heritage'.

Those photographs of the early murals were the first of what is now a collection of more than 20,000 images, of which more than 6500 are available in an open-access online archive, 'The Murals of Northern Ireland 1979–2017', hosted at the Claremont Colleges Digital Library. The murals were produced from within a war and they constitute a form of public art that has played an important role in Northern Ireland during the conflict and the post-conflict periods; they stand as a highly complex body of work. Many of the images draw on relatively stable and communally recognisable ways of making meaning, familiar to anyone who lives in Northern Ireland, specifically in the use of established symbolic forms and conventions (King William of Orange on a white charger, James Connolly outside the Dublin General Post Office in 1916). Yet many more of the murals embody highly contingent structures of feeling in their articulation of perceptions, stances towards, and affective responses to, history as it developed.

In truth the murals took many, often surprising, forms: some rallied support for Republican and Loyalist paramilitaries, while others denounced them; some addressed British soldiers directly (one in the form of a poem), while others were changed or defaced by soldiers to taunt Republicans; some voiced a longing for peace, while others made specific political demands; some declared international solidarity, while others expressed a local, sometimes very local, sense of belonging. In fact, with all the murals, even those that really were simple expressions of political viewpoints, their location, timing, and form, meant that they served intricate, often coded, purposes. For as well as expressing content, they also functioned to delineate spatial boundaries, to create modes of identity, to construct places of memory, to forge popular morality, and to establish collective sentiment. In short, although the murals were often striking works of art in their own right, they also had social and political significance and provide a unique perspective on the remarkable, complicated and difficult history from which they were created.

One of my colleagues rather unkindly remarked that 'basically, you've been standing in the pissing rain in Northern Ireland for forty years taking pictures of walls'. He wasn't wrong, although, evidently, there was a lot more to it than that. Photographing the murals involved gaining a detailed knowledge not simply of geographic space—from hauntingly desolate urban estates to picture-pretty rural villages, from Londonderry/Derry to Crossmaglen—but also of the social and cultural landscape of Northern Ireland (including its intricate and intimate sectarian boundaries). It has also meant engaging with a network of formal and informal contacts, from major political figures to community centre caretakers, from ordinary people in the street to the many muralists—of all persuasions—whose work I have recorded. And of course, it has entailed meeting the paramilitaries and the armed representatives of the State.

At the height of the conflict at least, being 'detained' by the para-militaries wasn't uncommon (nor unexpected—as one of them once said to me, 'only an idiot walks round here with a camera'). Nor was it excessively threatening, although being arrested by Loyalists was much more difficult than being lifted by Republicans because of the different relative political structures. Both sides soon lost interest once it'd been established that I was indeed just an idiot with a camera. Dealing with the 'security forces', on the other hand, was a bit trickier, and in the early days I lost a lot of film (it was the pre-digital era) to soldiers who just opened up the back of the camera to destroy the images (they didn't like people taking pictures of Republican murals). And the only time I was battered was by a policeman who lost his temper on Republican Springhill Avenue in Ballymurphy; given that the Provisional IRA had just tried to shoot him, it was, I suppose, understandable.

Given the context—the tension, the violence, the cynicism of the politics, and, incessantly, the rain—I have often been asked why do it? Why keep on going back to record the murals over such a long period of time? One answer, I suppose, is simple, good old-fashioned curiosity and a desire to understand the endlessly complicated history and culture of Northern Ireland with all its ancient scars. But why Northern Ireland (there are after all plenty of murals in all sorts of locations all around the world, most of which are less rainy and cold)?

Perhaps the proper response to that has to be because the horrible, appalling, tragic war that took place there reveals most clearly the politically-motivated violence that underpins democratic civil society, to which, most of the time, we, its prime beneficiaries, are blind. In other words, because the recent history of Northern Ireland embodies that fascinating paradox that lies at the heart of Hobbesian social theory (first articulated not long after Fanshawe's ode was published): that in order to guarantee our security and well-being, we give up the right to violence and entrust it to the State, but that if the State does not guarantee our security and well-being, we have the right (for Hobbes the necessity) to resort to violence.

And yet, of course, that wasn't the primary reason for standing in the pissing rain, sitting with paramilitaries, and negotiating the ever-present dangers posed by children and dogs. Because in the end, the reason I traipsed the length and breadth of Northern Ireland to record those images wasn't to satisfy my intellectual curiosity, nor to learn political lessons. I did it because the murals, even in their crudest forms, stand as testimony to the fact that even from the dead ground, even in the deepest, darkest, worst of times, when Northern Ireland was a world beyond the world, people, many of whom were working-class men deeply engaged in the war, expressed themselves through aesthetic form.

Often self-taught, or with the artistic skills that they had acquired in prison, they stood and painted maps of time and place on the walls of their communities. Sometimes the images were simplistic, crude, or silly; sometimes they were provocative, sectarian or shocking; sometimes they were highly wrought, complicated or historically resonant. And sometimes they were aesthetically accomplished. Incomprehensibly, perhaps, given that war was all the world about, the muralists made art, the beautiful'st of things. It was worth standing in the rain to ensure there was a record of that plain historical fact.

Loyalist mural, Ohio Street, North Belfast, 1987

Loyalist mural, Mount Vernon, North Belfast, 2001

Loyalist mural, Hopewell Crescent, West Belfast, 2014

Loyalist mural, Northland Street, West Belfast, 2016

Loyalist mural, Percy Street, West Belfast, 1987

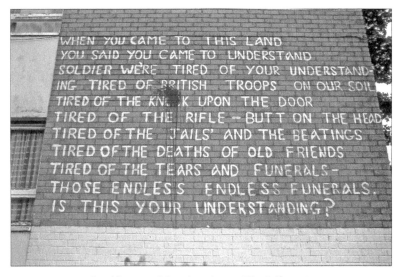

Republican mural, Lenadoon Avenue, West Belfast, 1981

Republican mural, Islandbawn Street, West Belfast, 1982

Republican mural,
Beechmount Avenue, 1996

Republican mural, McQuillin Street, West Belfast, 2016

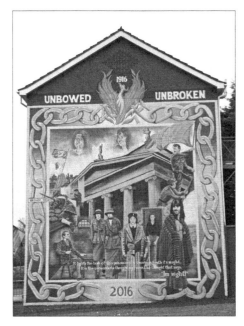

Republican mural, South
Link, West Belfast, 2016

John Brannigan

Border

IT IS A MOMENT of fleeting amusement to my children on the car journey to visit their grandparents, as we turn south of the ring of hills around Newry, to guess the precise point at which we pass, invisibly and silently, from one country to another. As we round Cloughoge Hill, nothing remains of the military architecture which once marked the British checkpoint here—the sangars, bunkers, barbed wire, and concrete blocks which made the hill look like a scene from the First World War.

Since the checkpoint was removed, the new motorway between Dublin and Belfast has been built over the same ground, carpeting over the bumps that used to indicate the change in road surface from North to South. A seamless, mundanely continuous road, it seems at odds with the apparent discontinuities and divisions of a border. You cannot see it or feel it, but it is there. An imaginary line, entirely credible and imperceptible, like the ones children invent on playgrounds every day. And so, the children perk up at Cloughoge, sit slightly forward, and survey the land ahead, judging distances to what might be, looking for the unknowable signs of what a border should look like. The middle child, who loves competitive games, sizes up the road signs. 'Now', he shouts, seizing on the sudden switch from miles to kilometres, or the appearance of Gaelic place names italicized above their familiar anglicized forms. Nothing besides remains to tell of this change.

In his book, *Border Foray* (1957), Richard Hayward recalls the 'boyish fun and curiosity' of the American GIs he had been tasked with escorting during the Second World War, who delighted in having their picture taken at this place with one foot in the North and one foot in the South, straddling a border they could not see. An Orangeman who spent much of his life promoting Irish song and theatre, Hayward took his own delight from straddling the border, and tells the story of stopping at the customs post, and knocking on the door for attention, only to be told by a farmer nearby, 'Sure there's no border at this time of the day: the man's away for his tay'.

Yet, even as he was writing, Hayward's comic depiction of a borderland of fiendish smugglers and outwitted lawmen was already out-of-step with the violence of the IRA border campaign of the 1950s, and he was dead before the war which erupted in 1969 would make much of his book seem frivolous and quaint. The same geography which made this place profitable and safe for smugglers, made it a killing ground. The names of the townlands which adjoin the border—Killeen, Meigh, Jonesborough, Drumintee, Kilnasaggart, Forkill—bonded in repetitive newspaper headlines with murderous words: shootings, booby traps, hijacking, snipers, landmines, ambushes. These townlands lay in the shadows between Slieve Gullion and Black Mountain, in the dead ground between the watchful border posts on either side.

The border of my childhood was never a single line, but two. At the foot of the Cooley mountains, as the forests gave way to grazing hills, the Gardaí and the Irish Army staged the first checkpoint. Soldiers lay in ditches, as if rehearsing an ambush. The Garda would grip the frame of the car door as he leaned in and asked where we were going. He had a country accent, and the hint of a grin, as if he could catch anyone out by just pretending to be mildly curious.

The other checkpoint on the British side could not be seen from here. We would leave one border behind, and enter the space between. The space between the checkpoints was a shallow bowl of gently undulating land, surrounded by hills and mountains on all sides. It was a choke point, the only natural passage through the difficult terrain which has historically marked the southern limits of Ulster.

Most of South Armagh was too dangerous for fixed checkpoints and road transport for the British Army and the RUC. They came and went by helicopter and foot patrols, and avoided the roads and the obvious stalking grounds. This stretch of road on the main Dublin to Belfast route was the most deadly section of the borderlands. Even after the erection of observation towers on Cloughoge Hill in 1986, the IRA conducted assassinations and ambushes in this area, taking advantage of dead ground and the paucity of patrols.

People could disappear here, even the soldiers most intent on knowing the land. They could be glimpsed in the bushes around the borderland, looking up from their maps, trying to read the terrain, then worrying at the maps again. In Eoin McNamee's *The Ultras* (2004), which gives a fictional account of the disappearance of Captain Robert Nairac in Drumintee in 1977, Nairac is depicted as obsessed with a map of the border:

> He drew lines on it, put small Xs beside isolated border
> farmhouses… Question marks were added, lines looped
> around geographical features for no discernible reason.
> Cryptic acronyms were added in a minute hand… He had
> a puzzled expression on his face, as if there were another,
> more detailed and clandestine legend elsewhere. One that
> gave reference points to the shifting nature of the place.
> The zones of infiltration. The cartographies of subterfuge.

In McNamee's novel, Nairac is a covert agent, half Cold War warrior and half boy-scout, who attempts to exploit the mystique of the border in the war against the IRA, but he becomes its victim, disappearing from a pub in Drumintee, never to be seen again. He became a 'clandestine legend', another story in the sinister lore of border warfare. His name was painted on backstreet walls and gables in towns and villages around the border, as a warning, as a lesson in the art of reading terrain.

The space between the checkpoints felt like a place apart, neither one territory nor another. It was a place of movement and exchange. The borderland abounded in haulage companies, shipping agents, customs handlers, currency exchange, pop-up fuel suppliers, and border-hopping sellers of all manner of taxable or prohibited goods. As Garrett Carr observes in *The Rule of the Land* (2017), there was always a look of impermanence about the businesses here, operating out of shipping containers and portacabins, even though they have been in the same place for decades.

Border people had deep roots, long histories of being settled in their own communities, in townlands so small that they hardly appeared on any but the largest scale maps. Yet they were extraordinarily proficient in the arts of movement, and the alchemy of cross-border exchange.

At Carrickcarnon, two nightclubs thrived, one on either side of the road, yards away from the borderline. Here at the weekends teenagers from Dundalk and Newry would meet to dance and drink, under the laser lights and the throbbing pulse of the music, until they were cast out into the darkness to find the buses waiting to bring them north or south. For a few minutes in the cold night air, some would walk north to the border. There were shouts, echoing in the hills, of 'Up the RA', and 'Fuck the Brits', hurled out into the dark space, to the rising road, and the unseen soldiers on sentry at the other side. On the bus home, rebel songs punctuated the seemingly inevitable chorus of 'You saw the whole of the moon'. The border could not but resonate with the songs of rebels and outlaws, or as Hayward calls them, *contrabandisti*.

In ancient times, this place was known as Bearna Ulaid, the Gap of Ulster, and more commonly now as the Gap of the North. It is one of the few natural gaps in the mountains and the drumlin belt which stretches from Down to Leitrim, and so, for as long as there have been records and stories of the people who live here, it has been a borderland.

In the *Táin Bó Cúalnge*, the seventh-century epic tale, many of the battles which take place between Cú Chulainn and Medb's army occur in these frontier lands. Indeed, much of the *Táin* is devoted to explaining the onomastic relationship between its stories and their settings. Local legend in the Slieve Gullion (*Sliabh gCuilinn*) area maintains still that the mountain derives its name from the blacksmith, Culainn, who lived on its slopes, and whose fierce hound was slayed by the boy who then offered to take its place, and so became known as Cú Chulainn (the hound of Culainn).

There are echoes of that hound surely still to be heard in the howls of the guard dogs which protect the scrap yards and warehouses dotted around the Gap. There are other echoes too. From the British Army observation posts which stood on Cloughoge, how often must the soldiers on duty have gazed down the valley to the remains of Moyry Castle, and wondered about the tragic and farcical repetitions of history? The castle, a mere defensive tower, was erected by Lord Mountjoy to overlook and garrison the Gap of the North in 1601, after his first attempt to quell O'Neill's Irish forces had been crushed here in a battle in which the Irish made use of every advantage of terrain, tactics, and weather.

O'Neill too had understood the value of dead ground, concealing his troops on reverse slopes, and luring Mountjoy's foot regiments in for the slaughter, surrounding them on three sides. The castle, like the watchtowers, were belated attempts to gain a griphold on treacherous terrain. It must have appeared then, as it appears now, as a symbol of order, but also of isolation.

From the windows of my classroom, we could watch the lumbering flight of the Wessex helicopters making regular supply drops at the outpost at Forkill. There were boys in that classroom who could speak knowledgeably about the point in its approach when the helicopter was most vulnerable, what weapons could bring it down, how many men would be needed to do so. There were boys who watched the slow hover of the Wessex every day, as if willing it to happen. The Wessex was a pregnant elephant of a helicopter with a large belly which could carry troops or supplies, and which sometimes lifted other equipment cradled beneath it, dangling over those dangerous Armagh hills. These were the necessary precautions of an army still islanded by geography, and by the invisible threats of 'bandit country', as it was called.

Outlaws had made a home of these hills since the time of Mountjoy, and long before, and were celebrated in songs and poetry. Gaelic customs and language survived here long after the nearby towns of Dundalk and Newry had become commercial, cultural and military centres of English rule.

In the eighteenth century, the poet-rapparee, Seamus Mac Murchaidh looked down upon Dundalk from Forkill, and wrote 'Is fuath liom an baile-cuain/ Dá ngoirtidhe Baile Mhic Buain/ Baile duairc gan chill gan chrois/ Nár théidim ann d'each nó do chois' ('I hate that harbour-town/ That was once called Baile Mhic Buain/ Morose town without church without cross/ I would not go there by horse or by foot'). Mac Murchaidh and his fellow-poet, Peadar Ó Doirnín, founded a school for Gaelic poetry in the townlands around Slieve Gullion in an attempt to preserve the bardic traditions of Gaelic culture, but they were repeatedly under threat of arrest and execution for their support of the Jacobite cause.

Mac Murchaidh's capture and hanging, probably around 1750, is commemorated in the song which consists of his own verses and those added by Ó Doirnín, and which laments that he cannot live on in some form in his homeland: 'Dá mbeinn i mo fhraochóig ar thaobh Bharr an Fhéadáin,/ nó dá mbeinn 'mo ghas raithní ar dheisiúr na gréine,/ dá dtéinn mar londubh go coillidh Dhún Réimhe/ agus thart go Carn Eallaigh mar ar tógadh le réim mé!' ('If I could be heather on the side of Fathom Hill,/ Or if I could be bracken in the sunshine,/ if I would go as a blackbird to the woods of Dunreavy/ and round to Carnally where I was reared with honour'). The song was reputedly sung at his wake, and has been sung in the area since.

The lie of this land inspires attachment as well as rebellion. Perhaps because of its frontier existence, and the constant motion of travellers, merchants, and armies through this narrow gap, local ties and pride are amplified between the hills. In Colm Tóibín's *Bad Blood* (1987), another account of walking the border, he concludes his narrative here, the scene of some of the worst atrocities and massacres of the Northern conflict, but also, in the words of one local, 'the most wonderful place in the world'. Garrett Carr speaks to locals who have the same strong sense of attachment and satisfaction, and he wonders amusedly if this can be attributed to the gravitational pull of the concealed and congealed volcanic rock beneath the surface of Slieve Gullion.

The folklorist, Michael J. Murphy, attributed his love of Gullion and its 'encircling acolytes' of hills to an 'earth spirit' in his lyrical essay, *Mountain Year* (1964). When I recall that passage between two checkpoints, there was always something magical, and something menacing, about this stretch of land. We were between countries, between armies, in a land seemingly made for smugglers, outlaws, and perhaps also for poets.

Rising up from Killeen, the road approaching the British checkpoint became more serious, funnelling cars into a torturous obstacle course of concrete pillars and ramps. There were the first glimpses of British soldiers camouflaged in the bracken, their faces smeared with paint, eyes intent along the sights of their rifles on distant shadows. Their poses seemed to imitate Airfix toy figures. The car was forced to slow, only the first in a series of necessary submissions. Red signs instructed the drivers to stop and switch off headlights. And then, as Seamus Heaney describes, 'The tightness and the nilness round that space/ when the car stops in the road'.

We were not what they were looking for, but the soldiers have to look, and have to ask, because they have learned not to trust anyone who crosses no-man's land. A soldier would relay the number plate into his radio, as if the car was the suspect and not the people inside. Another would lean into the car window, and ask questions with an accent which was immediately both strange and familiar. Glaswegian perhaps, or Yorkshire: accents we would know to mimic when we had left the checkpoint safely behind. I could identify some of the regiments from their berets or insignia—the paratroopers, the marines, the Scots regiments—from the stories and films and games about World War Two which pervaded my childhood.

I grew up fascinated by tales of their heroism in Arnhem, Bordeaux, and the beaches of Normandy. The same stories must have captivated the soldiers stationed at Cloughoge checkpoint when they were children too, and perhaps, like me, they had cause to wonder how one idea of the British Army was connected to the other. These soldiers had crossed borders, from the comic book pages of *Commando* and *Victor*, to a war with no heroes, no glory, and no victories.

They have left almost nothing behind. On the hillside of Cloughoge, a fading H on a tarmac square marks the place where the helicopters used to land. There are tracks still marked on the hill which might have been left by the soldiers, or maybe those tracks were older yet. The bunkers and sangars have been bulldozed into oblivion. The ghosts of Mountjoy's garrison can now look north from Moyry Pass, with no metal watchtowers to return their gaze. Every effort has been made to erase the appearance of a border.

On what remains of the old Dublin to Belfast road at Killeen, in almost the exact spot where a bomb killed four members of the RUC in 1985, and another, two years later, killed a Judge and his wife, and another, the following year, killed a married couple and their six-year old son, a large billboard now bears a campaign poster which reads 'Border Communities Against Brexit'. Against all the talk in London and Brussels, wily or wishful, of 'frictionless', 'seamless', or 'virtual' borders, these words seem to bear the weight of memory, of the histories of the people who have lived and walked and loved this land.

As I pass this poster with my children, still pondering where to locate the border, I wonder at the beautiful paradox of that phrase, 'border communities', at how it demands us to rethink our notion of peripheries and heartlands, at how it reimagines community out of a history of conflict and division. I understand now, as we pass from north to south, as we will later cross back again, as we have done so many times before, that my children are border children, and that perhaps we all belong to border communities.

Damian Walford Davies

Paradise Destroyed

To Wilton House

So Donne and Yeats and Landor were left in the quiet room
With the gentle ghost that had fellowed me so long.
And I passed to the sunlit bay, and the laughing waves
To site the guns in the heather, and reckon the battered odds
Of the first war shamefully ended, and the second unbegun
(For the thorns were not yet ripe on the sands
                    nor the dragons' teeth sprung on the beaches)
And we could talk on the terrace at night, drinking the wine,
Letting the mind flow easy between us four.

                    My friends were there:
Dick, the gallant, the courteous, carefree and angry,
A thousand years of England grown into his side,
Who went to stand between his village and the sea
Asking only that he might be placed in the front of the battle to
    come.
And the Guardsman, grey-haired and lean, blue-tanned from the
    desert sun,
Steel-straight, laughter in the grey eyes: who followed me
To the stone house by the River, and kept my mirth alive.
John Dain from his school desk; Patrick who spoke all tongues;
And all that gallant company—Norway Poland Holland Flanders,
    from the torn beaches—
Re-tempering after defeat.

Then in a moment flung
To the high room where the Van Dycks watch the maps
(Half a million rifles guarding King Charles' country)
And the beaches marked blood-red.
Above, the winged horse, and the maiden bound to the rock,
Watch us and wonder from the curved ceiling.
And I lie awake on the mattress, reckoning it all.
—All the folly and waste of the sunlit empty beaches, and the torn
     roof-trees,
—All the horror that follows the dark keel at night
—All the monuments broken with fire
—All my beautiful dead men.
The winged horse snorts above, and the planes move,
Engine calling to engine, declaring His power, through the stabbing
     lights.

                    (Whose invisible worm?)
But the Palladian Bridge guards the River
     and the gun-pit guards the Bridge
     and the trout hang poised in the shallows above the weir
     and the moon lights up the River to guide the enemy home.
Whom do I sup with tonight? (The Pleiades are gone.)
Yeats and Donne and Landor—three races and three men—
Guard me from the terror by night, and my own thoughts worst of all
In the blackness of the night.

                    What do new friends avail?
What mask do I wear? (Ophelia's mind o'erthrown.)
What valediction forbids mourning?
                    There's no constancy in the compasses:
The iron turns not west for any stone.

Only Inigo Jones, and the shadowed lines that he drew
And Sidney's tales of Shepherdesses as he walks outside
(Zutphen far off)—that white flame still a-fire—
And Touchstone jesting on the lawn outside.

Only the Epitaph stands.

But the moonlight's still on the River, and the engines overhead.
In this great room where all the past looks on
Can I not match an elegy to show
That dust grows angry with its blood and state
And all futilities dissolve again?

Arithmeticians, we?

Come, my Captains, for the blossoming night
Grows red and angry, and the worm's abroad.
Wheels mesh in the machine.

Tentatively titled '? Lament for the Beaches' and dated 'Sept. 1940' in typescript, this neglected late-modernist poem by T. R. Henn (1901–1974), first published in 1964 in the slim volume *Shooting a Bat*, takes its place in a distinguished tradition of English country house poems that includes such works as Ben Jonson's 'To Penshurst' and Andrew Marvell's 'Upon Appleton House'. Written a few months after Dunkirk by an Anglo-Irish Second Lieutenant serving as an Intelligence Officer at the headquarters of Southern Command at Wilton House (the Wiltshire seat since the mid-sixteenth century of the Herberts, Earls of Pembroke), Henn's poem is both eulogy and elegy. The country house poem was always troubled by history; a hymn to a house was necessarily a meditation on deracination as well as at-home-ness, political turmoil as well as dynastic stability and continuity. In 'To Wilton House', under the pressure of global war, harrowing personal guilt and a literary imagination bent on seeking connections between estranged but at the same time intimately related locations, the tradition is taken into new formal and psychological territory. In a room full of military maps, the speaker ironically struggles to orientate himself as the apparent certainties of Wilton and its park and estate dissolve in restive allusions to a literary tradition available now only in troubled parentheses, snatched shorthand.

At the centre of it all is the thirty-eight-year-old Henn, whose career as a Cambridge English don had been interrupted by the war. Written at a time when invasion seemed a certainty, and defeat more than likely, Henn's poem struggles to ground itself in what W. B. Yeats (whose reputation Henn was to play such a crucial role in establishing) calls 'one dear perpetual place'. 'To Wilton House' is a war poem; it is also a meditation on the dead ground of a place, out west, that Henn had left more than twenty years previously, whose history, values and subsequent fate remained formative and creatively troubling (indeed, traumatic). At the heart of 'To Wilton House' is the personal pain embodied in another, unnamed and unnameable, great house.

In the Double Cube

The 'high room' to which Henn refers is Wilton's exquisite 'Double Cube'. It is one of the great rooms of England, created by Inigo Jones and John Webb around 1653. Its dimensions—60 feet long, 30 feet wide, 30 feet high—are an incarnation of the order and perfection of the Wilton paradise. Wilton's association with Sir Philip Sidney (*Arcadia* was written in the grounds), with the poetry and patronage of his sister Mary, Countess of Pembroke, and with Shakespeare (*As You Like It* is said to have been played there in 1603 before King James—hence the poem's reference to Touchstone) established the arcadian mythos of the place.

As Henn revealed in his autobiography, *Five Arches* (1980), it was in this resonant space that he found himself playing 'endless war-games' and 'anti-invasion exercises'. On a trestle table in the Double Cube, which served as the operations room, was pinned 'a one-inch map of

Southern England, covered with talc' with 'the beaches … marked in red strips varying in width according to their vulnerability to invasion'. 'I was acting on the night of the 15/16th September [1940]', Henn recalls,

> when the wind and tide seemed right for the [German] invasion. It was an unforgettable experience, at night in the Double Cube under the curved painted ceiling, taking the signals as they came in every five minutes or so.

The poem offers a fleeting inventory of the Double Cube's embellishments and of the major landmarks in Wilton's demesne—the Palladian Bridge and the 'stone house by the River' known as the Daye House (once a dairy), home of the novelist Edith Olivier (1872–1948), with whom Henn lodged. As the poem notes, in one of the panels of the richly decorated ceiling is a representation of Perseus and Pegasus swooping to rescue the writhing Andromeda from the bestial enemy (a parable of war). Henn's inventory threatens always to become nightmarish phantasmagoria in which myth and murderous reality are intertwined. The flying horse metamorphoses into German bombers and reconnaissance aircraft which were 'returning from the Midlands' using 'the Avon as a landmark'. Henn's wife and children were at this very moment crossing to America to escape the bombers. The drone of their engines forms the descant to the poem.

With his fellow officers, Henn pores over maps that are also silently surveyed in the poem from the vantage point of history by the figures in Van Dyck's paintings (for which the Double Cube is also justly famous). The most celebrated of these is the portrait (1634/5) of the 4th Earl of Pembroke and his family, in which dead and soon-to-be dead children and an estranged, absent-looking wife flank a paterfamilias who looks utterly exhausted. It is a painting in which the Herbert family is strangely sited on the threshold of their own house, neither inside nor out. An anxious, similarly drained Henn would have recognised the contemporary personal and political relevance of the allegory.

Van Dyck represents a civilization both grounded and unhoused. *Et in Arcadia Ego* (it is Death who speaks): 'I also am in Arcadia'.

'To Wilton House' agitatedly summons not only the topography of the surrounding demesne but also the dead grounds of Europe, past, and passing, and to come. Zutphen in Holland is here, where Philip Sidney was shot in 1586 (he died, utterly unromantically, of gangrene three days later). Invoked in the reference to 'torn' and 'empty' beaches are the recent miracle of Dunkirk and the beach battles to come, for which Henn was specifically planning. The poem insists on friendship and fellowship: his officer-companions, profiled in the poem in a method learned from Yeats, are all identified in Henn's MS notes; the poem's first version contains a further roll-call of subalterns and superiors. However, this community is a fragile affair. The poem devolves into lonely terror, bracketed off in what becomes a psychological and stylistic tic ('my own thoughts worst of all').

Paradise (County Clare)

'All history was in the place,' Henn would later say of Wilton. All *his* history is here, too, and Wilton is haunted by a conditioning *elsewhere*. Both poem and Double Cube have charts at their centre, and the poem's attempt to map and record a threatened paradise is clear. Less obvious is the way the poem is also mapping *Paradise*—the name of Henn's family home, situated just south of Ballynacally at the junction of the Fergus and Shannon in County Clare, Ireland.

The Henn family—like the Herberts of Wilton, originally from Wales—had been established in Ireland since the late seventeenth century. At Paradise, the Big House (the usual designation in Ireland for country houses of the Anglo-Irish Ascendancy) displays in stone a family crest dated 1685. Henn's relationship with that house and estate crucially conditioned his identity and personality. Paradise is no Wilton; and yet, like the Arcadia of the Wiltshire earls, it was a place of privilege, circumscribed and self-contained, an idyll sustained by an ethnic and class mythology.

Five Arches profiles Henn's childhood at Paradise, the 'bountiful, erratic, wasteful' economy of the house, the 'quasi-feudal' structures on which it was based, the 'Conservative and Unionist' allegiances of his family of lawyers, churchmen, academics and soldiers, and—central to a reading of 'To Wilton House'—the economic forces and civil unrest that assailed Paradise following his father's death in 1915.

Throughout Henn's autobiography, the house is located in relation to the Protestant Big Houses that were burned by the IRA during the Irish War of Independence, the Civil War and the uneasy 1920s (which Henn refers to as 'The Troubles'). Though raided on numerous occasions by the IRA (and also by Free State troopers), Paradise was saved from fire at this time, Henn states, by his mother's 'courage and gaiety, and the respect of the people for her'. That said, the teenage Henn, on return visits from school at Aldenham, Hertfordshire and from Cambridge, kept 'a Spanish 9mm automatic pistol … cocked under [his] pillow at night'. As his poem 'Dark Journey' testifies, when there was 'a rumour of a raid', he used to beat the bounds of Paradise in the dark, rifle in hand, like an armed Protestant Adam hunting the republican serpent.

Henn was an Anglo-Irish scion whose world-view was inescapably moulded by all that Paradise, with its walled garden, home farm, private burial ground and loyal tenantry, represented. References in his *Last Essays* to the 'excitement, comedy [and] element of picturesqueness of speech and behaviour' provided by his family's domestics, and in *Five Arches* to the 'seemingly incessant Masses' to which the Paradise servants were taken by coach-and-jennet clearly betray his colonialist mentality (also instilled by his 'Indian interlude' with the Burmah Oil Company in Calcutta before the war). However, Henn also diagnosed with clarity the ills and demise of his own cultural and political class, and the rise and (necessary) fall of the Protestant Ascendancy Big House in a chapter in his book on Yeats, *The Lonely Tower* (1950). The poet who in 'To Wilton House' is acutely sensitised to the brittleness of Wilton's Arcadia and of the whole Anglosphere in the early autumn of 1940 knew well that his Paradise was founded on historical accident, expropriation and violence—as were England's great estates.

Assisting him in that realisation was his master, Yeats, with his own ambiguous relation to the custom, ceremony and courtesy of the 'levelled lawns and gravelled ways' of the Big House. 'Whatever the wrongs of past history on either side, this civilization that I had known as a boy was founded on something approaching serfdom,' Henn confessed; 'it seemed to me right that three centuries of Irish aristocracy had served their turn in history.' He was demythologising himself.

By 1940, Paradise, County Clare, was as good as lost. In the early 1930s, Henn had found his mother in her old age 'wandering in her night-clothes, candle in hand, through the long corridors, looking for the fires that treachery might have begun in some remote corner.' Boarded up, put up for sale, its manicured demesne breached by the Shannon's killing tides, the house would soon take on a 'blind' look. Henn's major poem 'Shooting a Bat' records what he encountered during one return journey: 'The funeral-windowed house, the leprous plaster,/ Half-kept—against what?'. He noted that from the mid-1940s onwards, 'the track of the transatlantic aircraft bound for or leaving Shannon' scored the sky above Paradise (not Heinkels, but nonetheless agents of modernity and internationalism that would see off eighteenth-century Ireland).

Guilt at his inability to redress the decline of Paradise and of the Anglo-Irish civilization it represented—his inability, he claims, 'to assume [his] Father's place'—resulted during the 1930s in a period of acute guilt and suicidal depression not fully exorcised when he came to Wilton. He had consulted Leonard F. Browne at the Tavistock Clinic and was told: 'Your heart is breaking.' Henn's memory of his father's coffin 'descending into the grave filled with snow and water' beside the windbreak fir grove overlooking the Shannon, south of Paradise, was the image that crystallised the pain. 'To Wilton House' is the mark of that trauma.

Paradise was sold to an absentee German owner in 1960; it burned down on the morning of 6 October 1970. It may have been the electrics, recently installed; it may also have been republican arson. Turning Yeatsian rhetoric to account, Henn's late poem on the demise of Paradise ('Burning of a House') names his civilization's sin: 'high ancestral arrogance'.

'The Iron Turns Not West'

Thus 'To Wilton House' is a celebration of and lament for Paradise, too. Touchstone may be jesting on the lawn outside the operations room (where Henn 'exercis[ed] with the Home Guard, using hand-grenades made of mud and bran and wooden rattles for machine-gun fire'). As the Second Lieutenant knew well, however, such clowning in the paradise of Arden brought home the very question of where home for Henn now was: 'Ay, now am I in Arden,' says Touchstone, 'the more fool I; when I was at home I was in a better place.'

Notable in the poem is a wished-for west. 'The iron turns not west for any stone,' Henn ruefully remarks. The reference, as his notes attest, is to America—the longed-for ally who had not yet entered the war (Donne's image of a pair of compasses becoming, over the line-ending, a magnetic compass), and the haven for which his family was heading. Crucially, Paradise, County Clare—out west—is here also, mapped as Wilton's dark and decaying Irish other, an Arden lost and 'shamefully ended'.

In another Wilton-centred poem, 'Fragments of a Testament', Henn refers explicitly to his ancestral house and County Clare as 'my own west coast'. In 'To Wilton House', however, Paradise is the structure that *cannot* be named. Introducing a section of his poems in *Five Arches*, Henn comments that 'after 1922[,] political events became almost too painful to settle or combine in the memory, except under pressure of real or imagined death.' 'To Wilton House' is desperately engaged in that act of 'combination' as it throws out geographical coordinates (local and global) and a flurry of semi-processed literary references—Homer, the Psalmist, Sappho, Sidney, Shakespeare, William Browne (author of the 1621 'Epitaph' to Mary Sidney), Donne, Blake, Landor, Whitman,

Yeats—in an attempt to *connect* and shore up a past, if only by means of textual detritus. Yet that reaching out merely confirms homelessness and a loss of identity. What 'mask'—the poem asks—does the Anglo-Irishman Henn wear in that operations room? Who is Tom Henn in the Double Cube?

'All the monuments broken by fire' are, of course, the marks of 'civilization' destroyed, and to be destroyed, by war and civil unrest. In Henn's cartography, those monuments are also Ireland's Big Houses—the 'anti-national' Palladian (like Wilton) edifices or grey three-storey Georgian structures that the Irish Free State's Office of Public Works and the 1930 National Monuments Act insisted were not 'monuments' at all. These buildings, odious symbols to the new state, were granted merely the textual courtesy of 'preservation by record' (an inventory of architecture and furnishings) before being demolished. Their ideological freight was too problematic. Thresholds, as Yeats said, gone to patch pig sties. At Wilton, 'The furniture and many of the pictures had been removed,' Henn remembered; at squatter-filled Paradise, 'the furniture and pictures [were] auctioned'. Henn's inventory in 'To Wilton House' has the force of a 'preservation by record' for two houses. At the poem's close, the 'red' and 'angry' flames of a deathly 'blossoming night' are those that would, three decades later—as Henn at some deep level knew—destroy Paradise.

Seamus Perry

Larkin's War

CYNICISM in Philip Larkin—as often, perhaps, in life—is usually a roundabout way of confronting a genuine difficulty of feeling by pretending that it is coarse and obvious; and so, by counter-suggestion, implying the complexity that is actually involved in a fuller and juster view. It is a way of being purposefully ugly, 'a hypocrite reversed' in Swift's great phrase—feigning yourself a morally smaller person than the situation demands, but also smaller than the person whom, really, you suspect yourself to be, or at least to be capable of being.

'Books are a load of crap': well, no, of course they aren't *crap*, and indeed Larkin's life was devoted to them, his own and others'; but at the same time, as Byron said, who would ever write who had something better to do? To say what Larkin says about books is risible; and yet you would clearly be wrong to think that the statement was somehow 'placed', as the critic F. R. Leavis used to say, dramatized purposefully to provoke our broader-minded objection to such an illiberal comment. Something serious is stirring in it, even if it isn't a serious proposition about the value of books. Larkin amusingly utilises the bluff plain-speaking public idiom of the 'Movement' manner; but, in a character-istically Larkinian way, the poem actually works to evoke the particular contortions of his own wholly private personality.

The seriously objectionable speaker of Larkin's poem 'Naturally the Foundation will Bear Your Expenses' is a study in the uses of such cynicism. Jetting off on another conference jaunt the speaker suddenly remembers that it is Remembrance Sunday only once his plane, irri-tatingly delayed by the gathering crowds, is well on the way to India: 'That day when Queen and Minister / And Band of Guards and all

/ Still act their solemn-sinister / Wreath-rubbish in Whitehall'. 'I've never written a poem that has been less understood,' Larkin told Ian Hamilton in an interview; but while it is a straightforward enough poem to construe, the feelings in the poem are in fact very difficult to understand, if that means making them line up in some coherent way.

'I hope it annoys all the continent-hopping craps,' Larkin wrote to Robert Conquest, who was one; but few readers can have thought the poem merely a satire on academics who enjoy the high life when they should be gratefully remembering the fallen. Larkin himself said to Hamilton: 'Why he should be blamed for not sympathizing with the crowds on Armistice Day, I don't quite know'—one of those memorable moments in his interviews when his own voice nears the timbre of his poetry (the end of 'Mr Bleaney', for instance: 'I don't know') as though catching some sort of more authentic utterance than normally allowed by the brilliant performance of being himself that he did for the interviewers.

At the same time, his most recent biographer James Booth quotes a letter Larkin once wrote to Monica Jones after listening to the Cenotaph service which suggests that Larkin's own emotions could be very far from lacking sympathy with the crowds: the sound of the Guards playing 'Nimrod' 'harrows me to my foundations', he told her.

Larkin didn't have what people of my parents' generation (which was also Larkin's) called a 'good war', in the way that his friend Kingsley Amis so manifestly did. He found the war work he volunteered to do during long vacations boring and humiliating: 'Our job is to reduce a Fucking Great Pile of Fuel Rationing forms into a Fucking Great Pile of Fuel Rationing forms arranged in (1) alphabetical order of streets, (2) those streets in numerical order… ' Indeed, you could say Larkin scarcely had a *war* at all; and it was a non-experience which, poetically speaking, was the making of him.

For Larkinian experience at its most characteristic is always closely related to not having had the experience you were expecting or for which you were hoping: it is a matter, often, of being on the edge of some great and moving and encompassing event but not really being part of it—looking at other people entering into the marriage you will never contract, or watching the young lover you never were, or gazing into a room of dancers whom you will never join. Larkin's war, in which he was not only non-combatant but in a curious and wilful way positively non-participant, was the origin of a whole poetic disposition. 'I don't feel "I lived through that",' he would later write to Monica of the war, remembering those times as though through someone else's eyes, 'I just feel "How wonderful!"'

He spent the war in Oxford studying English at St John's College, initially going about his life under the assumption, shared by all his contemporaries, that his time would soon be up and that conscription would come. In the meantime Oxford was not Oxford but an odd, pinched diminishment of itself, with rationed wine and food and life, and more and more dons and students missing: 'There was not a great deal of scope for personal development in the sense of high living along the *Brideshead* lines,' as he later put it in a characteristic piece of drollerie. 'Of course, the war's mucked everything up,' John's old teacher tells him in the Oxford wartime novel, *Jill*. 'Army lorries thunder down Cornmarket Street in an endless procession,' Larkin wrote rather fruitily to a school friend, 'in the depths of the university quadrangles, I gain the impression of being at the end of an epoch.' The sense of an ending was repeated: 'At the end of every term somebody left,' he wrote in the reminiscent preface to the 1975 re-issue of *Jill*.

Somebody—but not Larkin, of course. He failed his medical board for myopia, news he learned on 1 January 1942 after having burned all his work notes on the assumption of his imminent departure. His immediate reaction: 'I think it releases me from most of the carnage,' he wrote, 'even if doesn't let me stay at Oxford,' which was very far from disappointment. He had never wanted to join up: 'I don't think I could ever fit happily into the army,' he told a combatant friend. He later recalled: 'Nobody could have been expected to understand that without being a conscientious objector I did not want to join the army on moral grounds,' a paradoxical thing to say since it is hard to see how a moral objection could fail to engage the conscience in some way. He claimed his to be a common feeling: 'I was fundamentally — like the rest of my friends — uninterested in the war'; but that was to attribute to a group what was really an incorrigibly private affair.

'Perhaps you think I am being a bit selfish but I just don't want to go into the Army,' he wrote to someone who was in the army: 'I want to pretend it isn't there: that there's no war on'; and he was of course aware that 'being a bit selfish' in such a way was not a sentiment in tune with public spirit or even national survival: 'Men must abide by their feelings — I can't help it if everyone were like me we s'd all be hung.'

Two not very good sonnets he wrote in 1940 contrast 'The Conscript', a reluctant soldier who discovers in Lawrentian mode that after army life there remains 'no core of life within his bud / To animate his thoughts of good and bad', with 'The Conscientious Objector', who fares no better, wandering off on a cold solitary journey like an exiled Anglo-Saxon, 'till, lost amongst the mist, / He falls amid cold logic's stalactites'. His editor, Archie Burnett, records that Larkin wrote above the first poem 'Tripey'; but the poems at least manage to express what is felt as an impossible quandary, in which no possible course of action is going to be any good.

The sense of a whole world of conflict of which one was obviously obliged to be conscious, but also of a vast corporate effort in which one could not share a part, for reasons that were hard to rationalise: this is the strikingly recurrent feature of his wartime writings. 'Externally, I believe we must "win the war". I dislike Germans and I dislike Nazis, at least what I've heard of them. But I don't think it will do any good': how strange to put 'win the war' in inverted commas, as though you were quoting the sort of thing other people said, instead of describing one historical outcome rather than another, while all the time you had some other quite private idiolect to nurture. And to *dislike* Nazis is tendentiously not to speak the language of oratory or public opinion: when victory came in Europe Larkin was repelled by the rhetoric of achievement: 'I listened to Churchill blathering out of turn this afternoon, and the King this evening. But all day I have had a headache and felt despondent. The second draft of the novel has reached p.22.'

It was not only complicated memories of his father's lasting regard for Hitler that lay behind such sentiments: 'I am more than ever certain that England *cannot* win this war: there's absolutely no *spirit* in the country. I feel everything is in a mess' (this sent to a serving soldier in April 1942). That note of strident imperviousness to anything like a national cause is pure Lawrence, a writer whom Larkin revered throughout his life. It is as though Lawrence showed at its best and most heroic something less simply admirable or even acceptable that Larkin found in himself: what he loved in Lawrence's rebarbative individualism was an intrepid and vivid version of his own unshiftable sense of just not fitting in happily anywhere, neither in the army nor anywhere else.

'For the major part of the year I have been filled with a sensation new to me — of being irrevocably cut off from the rest of man,' he wrote towards the end of the war, and predicted that his fate was '[to] grow sourer and sourer.' Well perhaps that is just what he did: it is some mitigation to say that several great poems came from it. Years later, after watching old wartime films in Hull, he wrote to Monica: 'The war films tended to leave me feeling as isolated as the war itself did — d'you think people really felt as they were supposed to? all these parades of landgirls & factory workers … I don't know … It seemed a civil service war, a trade union war. I don't know.' ('I don't know.') Amis, in the Signals, never saw a hostile shot fired, but he had had a *war*, and although his nerves were left in shreds by his experience, he could nevertheless look forward to a life. 'A very good preparation, the Army,' says one of his characters in a short story. 'For what?' he is asked. 'For everything,' he replies.

Another Amis narrator says: 'It is true, I thought, that the Army would lick anyone into shape. You could even say that it made a man of you'—which Amis does not say without a sardonic edge, of course, but also not without a genuine sense of endorsement. Nothing ever made a man of Larkin in that way.

When James Joyce was asked what he did in the first war he replied that he wrote *Ulysses*; and Larkin could have said that he wrote *Jill*, but he wouldn't have. Amis may have had in mind the pointed contrast in their wartime experiences when he wrote to Larkin that he had enjoyed the novel, 'adding that its binding reminded him of *Signal Training: Telegraphy and Telephony*, or possibly *Ciceronis Orationes*' (as Larkin recalled in the preface to the reissue of *Jill*); and the sense of difference flashes elsewhere: in one his short stories, Amis's surrogate receives a letter from 'a friend of his in Oxford, one who, like most of his contemporaries, was medically unfit for military service — a doubly fortunate shortcoming in the present case, for one of his friend's several neuroses forbade him to be ordered about. The letter was full of undetailed assertions of hatred and misery…'

Larkin's neurotic war was spent, as he says in a sweet-tempered late poem to Monica, in an Oxford that still 'holds us, like that *Fleae* we read about / In the depths of the Second World War' ('Poem about Oxford'). But his war was not without terror. Reading Donne in the depths of a war celebrates the value of the poetical while still allowing for the unignorable pressure of historical events; and that this particular flea ends up crushed is perhaps not such a great omen. 'I think it's important not to feel crushed,' he told Ian Hamilton.

Yet Larkin would go on to find his greatest subject in crush, in damage; and the formative experience of damage was undoubtedly seeing his home town, Coventry, after the first bombing in November 1940—'Raids of last Tuesday simply buggered our district to Hades'— when he was still uncertain about the survival of his parents, an episode he memorably re-creates in *Jill*. An early poem, 'A Stone Church Damaged by a Bomb', possibly about Coventry Cathedral (where he had been baptized), makes the link between bomb damage and mental damage in its one memorably great piece of phrasing: 'what scaffolded mind / Can rebuild experience…?'; and the spirit of the poem goes on, as Andrew Motion suggests in his biography, to shape later poems in which the war doesn't explicitly figure at all, such as 'Church-Going' and 'The Explosion'.

I would say much else besides: I don't think he ever got over that episode. When in his funny and cantankerous *Memoirs* Amis wrote about the late Larkin poem, 'Love Again', which speaks of the permanent effect of 'violence / A long way back', he affected to be perplexed by his friend's wording: '*Violence?*' As though to say: what violence was there ever in *Larkin's* life? The poem is assiduously discreet in ensuring there is no obvious answer, but the destruction of Coventry from the air is surely a big element within it, an aspect of a war in which Larkin was both wholly implicated and yet compulsively self-excluding.

Peter Stothard

Henry *versus* Herbert

IN THE YEAR that I left school we were marking merely the fiftieth anniversary of the end of the First World War. There was little enthusiasm for this then from anyone that I knew.

For the older masters at Brentwood School in 1968 the war had not quite ended. It was a risk for a pupil to suggest otherwise. The eleventh hour was still in the Essex future, the eleventh day still the day after tomorrow, the eleventh month too far away for calculation.

As for the older pupils, we were keen to be free to grow our hair and join the students of peace protest. We were tired of our school of war, our red brick classrooms in our Memorial Hall, our grounds that were a permanent reconstruction of the Somme, endless and flat, the school glider scouring its few places to hide.

We did not need an anniversary. We already knew our place in history. We knew the trenches that had once lined the junior lawn, the sandbags under the stage, the gas masks for the whole town that the headmaster held (fee-paying boys first), the eigthy per cent of brave OBs who became officers, the evacuees who arrived from east London, our boys having classes in the morning, theirs in the afternoon.

Sometimes our classics masters could be even more ambitious than our modernists in connecting us to the past. One of them liked to boast a Battle of Brentwood during the Roman invasion of Britain in 43 AD, an event otherwise told exclusively by Robert Graves in a novel.

Both modern wars were essentially the same war in Brentwood, arguably the ancient ones too. In 1914 the the trenches had never reached us but that was merely good fortune. In 1940 the cricket pavilion had been hit by an oil bomb, a defeat of almost sporting proportions. In any future land battle for Brentwood, at any time after 1968, the Huns would have to overcome barbed wire around the cricket pitches, boys and masters on night patrol, flag signals on the clock tower, and most of all our elite air brigade.

We would not concede easily. Half of our masters held military ranks, satisfyingly inflated from those they had earned in war service, different levels too for when they were in the reserves or in the Combined Cadet Force, 'the oldest CCF of any school in the country', or maybe 'the second oldest'. All rankings were good and our gliders were as all-conquering as our soccer team.

War poetry would help to make us strong. We read from the now unfashionable second half of Virgil's *Aeneid*, the manual of permanent imperial war which the Romans would surely have brought to Brentwood even if they had not stopped to fight. The old fuelled the new.

We were encouraged towards the now little read Sir Herbert Read whose epic, *The End of a War*, was about just what it said, 'a' war, one of many, an event to be endured and probably repeated. There were few ranking points for Robert Graves, none at all for Wilfred Owen, Rupert Brooke and others now known as 'the war poets', who saw their sufferings as unique and made such 'a fuss'.

The headmaster was sometimes criticised for this by younger colleagues. He cited W. B. Yeats as sharing his view. Some of the dissidents also read selectively from Henry Reed, the hero of the Second World War anthologies, the poet who turned weapons training into art. Sometimes the headmaster confused the two men.

* * *

My favourite among the younger masters was known to us as Flt Lt, Flight Lieutenant Featherstone, who twirled a moustache and taught both gliding and art. The two were as one to him. It was astonishing, he said, what we would see from a glider, despite ours being hardly more than a wooden toy, fired like a catapult shot from a giant rubber band.

I discovered he was right. Within the endless flat outfields where our model armies tramped were hollows invisible from the ground, hiding places for boys in less than full uniform, girls too, the caretaker smoking, the school house matron (yes, almost certainly) with the master of the junior gym. That was all on my very first flight, a glimpse of 1968 from the sky.

Flt Lt did not believe that any war had been won on the playing fields of Brentwood, still less that there had ever been a Battle of Brentwood outside the pages of fiction. But nothing was more important, he said, than not being seen and knowing that one could not be seen.

'The Romans understood that particularly well,' he explained. If we wanted to think beyond fifty years from the Somme, we could consider the Battle of Colchester, the Roman victory that ended the Emperor Claudius's brief campaign to conquer the easy parts of Britain.

He was planning a final school trip. For the purposes of this lesson, and only this lesson, Art stood for Artillery. If anyone in his class 'cared to listen' to him at ten o'clock on Monday morning he would say more.

If we cared to listen? Choose to go or not? Flt Lt was a realist. In 1968 we were already beyond compulsion. We had our futures secured— in Oxford or the Ford Motor Company, in Cambridge or insurance. The Huns—our name for the few brave boys who chose German over Greek—were offering a rival trip to a brewery.

*   *   *

But we were curious and we came to the art room, punctually at 10.00. The sand in the egg-timer by the door had not yet begun to fall. On a blackboard in a corner, hidden as though it might or might not be part of our lesson, was a diagram of a tall tube beside a small triangle.

An arrow pointed from the second to the first, possibly an explanation of condom use, I wondered. Our sex education, in as much as its theory was taught at all, had been delayed until we were almost free of the hollows where so much practice took place.

'Wave Lift over a mountain,' said Flt Lt, maybe having realised the potential for misunderstanding. 'The air stream hits the peak, dips and soars, taking the glider to the greatest heights that a glider can reach.' He pointed to the tip of the tube: 'Up to 40,000 feet if the pilot has the guts to hang on.'

He seemed as flustered as if my sexual explanation had been correct. 'Not to be confused with Ridge Lift or Thermal Lift, not that we can do any of them here. Essex is much too flat.'

A range of voluntary art activity was on offer. In the opposite corner from the blackboard the singer and the drummer of the school band began stencilling what was then called psychedelic script, bulbous Os and Vs, in pale pinks and purples. The singer wore mirrored glasses. His collaborator looked as though he had already started work on the Transit Van.

Most of us preferred the chairs closest to the exit. Flt Lt lifted a chalk-duster. Instead of hurling it as once he would have done, his hand and voice subsided. 'When we go to Colchester next Tuesday, we will meet here at 9.15, each of you with a packed lunch. No oranges.' The banning of oranges was as much a part of Brentwood tradition as training for British air power, its origins owed to a mythical accident experienced by a previous headmaster.

Flt Lt turned away and faced the blackboard. As soon as the waves and ridges were dusted to smears, be began drawing concentric circles, rather more evenly than the amateurs of psychedelia at the other end of the room. He marked out the route up the hill to what is now Colchester castle. He spelt our destination in capitals, cross-hatching several segments.

'These,' he said, 'were the parts that the commander could not see, where the enemy might be hiding, where his own scouts might have hidden without his knowledge. Even the flattest battle field contained the visible and the invisible. Nothing was more important than to understand which was which.'

What precisely was Flt Lt's point? His voice was clear and flat as his ideal landing strip but why was he telling us this? Those of us at the artillery end of the art class began to look enviously at those lettering LOVE in water colours. 'The Romans,' he went on, 'were masters of reading terrain.'

'Without knowing what could not be seen, a commander could not judge distances.' He paused and took a slim buff-coloured book from his desk.

'Perhaps you may never get the knack of judging a distance,' he read. 'But at least you know how to report on a landscape: the central sector, the right of the arc.'

I looked to the right with embarrassing obedience. I did not at first notice that he was reciting. We were used to our teachers passing off others' words as their own. The promoter of the Battle of Brentwood did it all the time.

'You must never be over-sure.'

He paused again. I stared. By the window the eyes of the letter painters began moving towards us rather than ours towards them.

'You must never be over-sure. You must say, when reporting: At five o' clock in the central sector is a dozen of what appear to be animals; whatever you do, don't call the bleeders sheep.'

The singer and the drummer came sheepishly from their window and sat with the rest of us in the centre of the room. Flt Lt ignored their arrival.

'The human beings, now: in what direction are they, and how far away, would you say? And do not forget there may be dead ground in between'.

Flt Lt put the book down. He looked up at the clock.

'The invisible is the dead ground,' he said to what was now almost all the class.

He repeated the words. He repeated them in the way that teachers used when we were meant to remember, the Dead and the Ground.

The sand in the egg-timer was chasing the clock to the destination of 11 o'clock. He moved the duster through the concentric circles.

'Soldiers who were looking over dead ground did not always know it was there. Those who were in dead ground did not always know how invisible they were.'

'That is why gliding changes everything. From a glider dead ground comes alive.'

The bell rang for 'break'. The last sand left the higher glass.

There was a tumbling down the stairs. The drummer asked the singer what the fuck all that reading was about. A Ford apprenticeship was awaiting him very soon.

The singer said he had looked at the book on the way out. The poems were called 'Lessons of the War', the author a man called Reed, Henry or maybe Herbert. He was recalling a recent rather confusing talk by the headmaster.

'Anti-war?' asked the drummer, clutching his LOVE album sleeve.

'I think so,' said the singer. 'Lessons, anyway. Lessons nearly always mean what you've got wrong. Lessons of my triumphs? Not something you often hear.'

'You think Feathers has finally lost it?'

'Hope so.'

'You going to Colchester?'

'No, I've been.'

*   *   *

I returned to school only once to see Flt Lt. By the sixtieth anniversary he had become a true man of Brentwood which was perhaps no surprise.

'So, yes, dear, Henry not Herbert, Henry always hated being confused with Sir Herbert Read.'

'Hmm.'

'Herbert was a poet of the First War, Henry of the Second, Herbert a bit of an an anarchist, very French, Henry much the more British and worked at the BBC.'

My master of art and gliding now gave the impression that he knew both poets personally.

'Isn't it providential,' he said, 'that the "Naming of Parts" and "Judging Distances", the finest poems to come from the last war, were written by a man who never fought at all.'

I nodded. At least after that last art class (the trip itself to Colchester never happened), I had read Henry Reed's 'Lessons of the War' for myself.

In a very few lines each lesson contrasts the military school life of weapons and targets with the gardens and fields of civil peace. The first begins: 'Today we have naming of parts. Yesterday we had daily cleaning.' It now appears in more anthologies than any other of its time.

The lesson partly read by Flt Lt in his last class was the second in the set: 'Not only how far away, but the way that you say it is important.' The poem leads firmly from the classroom to the world beyond, where space is measured by time, direction by 'five o'clock in the central zone' and where humans embracing in the distance may only appear to be lovers, grazing animals only possibly sheep, and their distance away 'about one year and a half', always allowing for 'dead ground in between'.

We were back in the art room. 'If we taught you anything about war I hope we taught you that.'

'Of course, Herbert Read, such a fine critic of the surrealists too, did fight in France.' Flt Lt continued his distinction between the two while pointing out of the window. 'He took the MC and DSO,' he added, describing the medals as though they were graduate degrees. 'Yeats thought him vastly superior to Wilfred Owen, him of all that awful "passive suffering".'

'I did my best to look more knowing than I felt while he went on.

'There was that rather bad *Oxford Book of Modern Verse* in the Thirties. Yeats was the editor and put in all his friends, no Robert Graves, who was too greedy for a large fee, hardly any Auden, nothing from *The Waste Land* and seventeen pages of dear Herbert who was very brave but a very bad poet.'

'The headmaster used to disagree,' I reminded. 'He thought Herbert Read satisfyingly anti-German, no friend of "the Huns" as we were taught to know our European partners.' Flt LT seemed not to hear and, with a tweak on his moustache, stumbled on.

'Herbert believed that the Great War in Europe was a bad thing but an ordinary thing, hard to avoid from time to time. The so-called War Poets thought it an exceptional thing. Henry was a great writer. You don't need to fight a war in order to produce poetry about it, often much better not to. Herbert was a bad writer but right about wars in Europe, I'm afraid.'

Alan Riach

This Savage Wood

IN EARLY November 1942, George Campbell Hay (1915–1984) sailed from the Clyde on a week-long voyage to Algiers, one of the many soldiers taking part in Operation Torch, the American-British advance against Rommel's desert army. While his fellow Gaelic poet Sorley MacLean (1911–1996) was wounded at El Alamein, Hay's company ventured further east, crossing the North African desert into Tunisia, where the fighting continued through to May 1943. Hay was to encounter civilians in Tunis and Bizerta and witnessed how they were caught in the crossfire and bombing.

Hay's time in the desert war began in frustration and despair. The frustration was first because his duties were, as he described them, those 'sometimes of an office-boy, sometimes of an amateur charwoman, sometimes of an unskilled stevedore.' He was 'loading and unloading lorries', 'filing away forms in number order', 'ruling lines on sheets of paper', 'looking after the Oxygen and Acetylene supply' and keeping records. His facility with languages, he knew, should have made him eligible for more appropriate work but the Intelligence Corps and the War Office had rejected him. He was an unofficial interpreter for his unit in French, Italian and Arabic, having picked up the last two languages since arriving in North Africa.

His status as a private soldier may have been because of his history of avoiding conscription and his continuing concern with conditions in Scotland, where he had heard that women were being forcibly removed to armaments factories in England. This led him to anxiety and bitterness: 'I think that the maiming or extinction of the Scots … is intended… I think of her as a nation against whom a white war, biological and economic, is being waged under this bloody war against Germany.'

Hay had grown up familiar with Gaelic, Scots and English, becoming a brilliant linguist and translator from Welsh, Irish, French, Greek, Italian and Arabic. His poetry in English, Scots and Gaelic crosses more boundaries and engages more forms and tones than any modern poet. This is what lies behind his unfinished epic 'Mokhtar and Dougall': an approach to questions of cultural difference and identity through the profound understanding of the languages of its characters. Written 1944–47, it begins with the two title characters dead on an African mountaintop, mouths filled with 'hot dust' after the 'hard voice of the mortar' ended their songs 'with splinters, roaring and smoke'. That emphasis on mouths, voices, sounds, is important.

What survived of this poem gives an account of Mokhtar, his immediate ancestors and the Arab world they inhabited in North Africa, including a searing narrative describing a journey across the Sahara by Mokhtar's ancestor, Omar. It's worth noting that Hay's poetic evocation of the desert has its counterpart in the modernist Scottish composer Erik Chisholm's one-act opera *Simoon* (1952; DCD34139 Delphian, 2016), in which the oppression of the sandstorm and the psychological as well as physical aspects of cultures at war, Arab and French, is incomparably powerful not only in the libretto from Strindberg's play but horrifyingly in the music itself. What is unfinished in Hay's poem is largely the history and story of Dougall, Mokhtar's Scottish counterpart. It's as if the evocation of the desert was intensified by the memory of his own Scottish childhood, and when coming to write the poem, that part of his own personal history which would have informed the poem was neglected and ultimately drifted away into silence. We'll return to this point.

As a boy, Hay lived in Tarbert, on the shore of Loch Fyne, going out with the fishermen and wandering in the woods and hills around the village. He was intimately knowledgeable and precise in his descriptions of the natural world, animals, birds, flowers and trees, and his literary and linguistic expertise was tempered by a social understanding of people in the community he belonged to. The fishermen grew to be close friends and their working economy was deeply familiar to him. In October 1940, in his twenties, Hay went into the hills of Argyll, avoiding conscription. He was stopped in Arrochar on 3 May 1941, imprisoned until reporting for service in June in the Royal Army Ordnance Corps. At Catterick, he met Sorley MacLean and according to MacLean, they 'had two splendid afternoons and evenings when we talked Gaelic poetry the whole time.'

'Why did the poets go to the desert?' The question is the opening of Edwin Morgan's poem 'North Africa' in his sequence *Sonnets from Scotland* (1984). He goes on to list Hay, MacLean, Hamish Henderson, Robert Garioch, G. S. Fraser and Morgan himself, all moving through the North African theatre of war. 'Africa is admirable,' Hay wrote: 'there is a general air of life and a tolerance in small details (probably due to poverty) which are lacking in industrialised N.W. Europe. There is none of the ugliness which is the rule by the Clyde or the Tyne: there is more of natural good manners and less of convention and there are also some very bizarre smells to be dodged here and there…' And further: 'With French, Italian and Arabic I can always find a welcome and interesting company wherever I go…'

Hay, MacLean and all these Scottish poets crossed each other's trails in the desert, and their very different stories after Africa belie the shared fact of their experience of that Dead Ground. Hay's experience there, though, is in one crucial respect distinct: for Hay, North Africa yielded a sense of a complementarity of cultures, cognate across differences, which doesn't so much polarise or neutralise anything as partialise it. It is not simply that death levels all, but that languages deepen and extend humanity. In this perception, Gaelic, English, Scots, Italian, French and Arabic, the African language-worlds he encountered, bring another dispensation, different from the arbitrary absolutes and polarities of war. The language-worlds of Gaelic, Scots and English made social life possible for Hay in his childhood and upbringing, and act as correctives to the polarising singularities of military engagement.

For Hay, no language could have absolute power. Writing his own poetry in Gaelic, Scots, English and other languages, Hay knew profoundly and intimately the value of complementarity brought to bear by different cultures, and that any one language was only a partial realisation of humanity's potential. This is what made his war so terrible, as he witnessed the destruction of Bizerta having heard the voices of people there, people he could imagine, unbearably close, their languages silenced in the bombs exploding in city streets and bringing the buildings down. Inevitably for Hay, the blitzing of that city would later recollect similar devastation at home in Scotland, both literally, in Clydebank, and more generally, in the ruination of Gaelic culture and the world he knew as a boy and young man.

So for Hay, the 'Dead Ground' was not only, or not simply, the African desert but rather the destruction of living human culture most evidently practised in silencing the variety of languages by which people of different identities might convey a common humanity to each other. If there is one poem from the whole era which delivers the sense of the devastation of human potential such warfare generates it is Hay's 'Bizerta': 'The blaze, a horror on the skyline, / a ring of rose and gold at the foot of the sky, / belies and denies / with its light the ancient high tranquillity of the stars.' The killing of people of other cultures and other languages is what carries the rage of 'Bizerta' and keeps Hay's poetry an unfailing resource of resistance, refusing surrender or acquiescence.

War polarises. One of its primary functions is to define otherness. In Hamish Henderson's phrase, 'There were our own, there were the others.' Henderson's *Elegies for the Dead in Cyreneica* begins with the question, 'Why should I not sing *them*, the dead, the innocent?' He identifies a collective, unifying mortality in 'the brutish desert'. A similar sense of levelling death preoccupied Sorley MacLean.

MacLean arrived in Egypt in December 1941 and was wounded twice before more serious injuries from a landmine explosion at El Alamein on 2 December 1942 sent him to hospital and then home. He talked to me once of his time in the desert, saying he did not mind so much the constant condition of war or the exceptional volume of sound produced by the explosions but the memory of the cold clear water of a particular loch on the Isle of Skye had never been in his mind and sensual memory more intensely than during that period. In his poem 'Under the Ruweisat Ridge' he depicts a German soldier lying killed in the sand, noting that none of the vaunted pride in death is visible in the corpse of the Nazi. Robert Garioch, taken prisoner at Tobruk, talks of his experience of the desert war and his memories of imprisonment are recounted in his prose memoir *Two Men and a Blanket* (1975) and his long poem, 'The Wire'. 'Letter from Italy' ends like this:

> Perimeters have bounded me,
> Sad rims of desert and of sea,
> The famous one around Tobruk,
> And now barbed wire, through which I look,
> Except above—the Pleiades.

All these poets settle on the equalising facts of mortal being and the cosmic context but Hay's poetic expression of common life in the Dead Ground is different.

Angus Calder once noted that the Scots' poems stand comparison with those of the major participant-poets such as American Randell Jarrell, German Johannes Bobrowski, Russian Boris Slutski, Greek Odysseas Elytis, Hungarian Miklós Radnoti and English Keith Douglas, and that each one focuses sharply on particular events in a vision where irony and tragedy come together. For MacLean, three different histories and imperatives are brought together in the war poems: 'that of a war fought needfully against Fascism and Nazism by a British Empire which MacLean detested, that of the Scottish Gaels, saturated in military tradition, and that of Scottish Calvinism, which had come to overlap so largely with Gaeldom.' The contrast with Hay is striking: for Hay, the same human drive to power was as characteristic of British as of German imperialism, and the military tradition of Gaeldom held no appeal. Hay's father was a Church of Scotland minister and a novelist but Calvinism, with its notions of the elect and the damned, was not part of Hay's sensibility.

His understanding of the common life of communication in the desert of modernity was earthed in his understanding of the dynamics of human nature in expression through different languages, and the sense of different cultural histories happening across generations and informing present life. This understanding opposes the polarisations of war.

In 'Mokhtar and Dougall', his broken epic, this is the structuring principle. It's revealing that the completed parts of the poem recount the lives of Mokhtar's immediate ancestors, father and grandfather, while those parts of the poem dealing with the Scotsman Dougall are unfinished, sketched, only suggested. It's as if Hay's own early biography and his subsequent, post-war long-term distress and long silence might have supplied the story that the mere cypher of Dougall's name implies. For Hay, the polarisations of war were meaningful because they introduced him to other cultures whose people he met and talked with, whose languages he learnt and absorbed, whose affinities across difference he endorsed. He embraced Muslim 'others' by learning their language and understanding how the articulation of consciousness in that language differed from and complemented his own Gaelic—as well as the Scots and English languages in which he also wrote his poems. The tri-lingual nature of his poetry intrinsically rejects the colonial purchase of the world through a monolingual apprehension and expression of it. In itself, it relativizes and opens dialogue.

This makes him a very different character from the poets of action, Hamish Henderson, Keith Douglas, and Sorley MacLean. They are poets of contemplation too, of course, but Hay's contemplative depth involved others in a different way.

In June 1944, his unit moved to Italy, based around Salerno and Naples. Ideas that had begun to take shape in Algeria found expression in an abundance of poems written at this time, including the beginnings of 'Mokhtar and Dougall' (with the grim opening and the vivid depiction of Omar's journey across the Sahara). In spring 1945,

Hay was promoted to corporal then sergeant, and in January 1946, was posted to Greece. He was a familiar figure among the local people in Macedonia, where political divisions and factions meant that such company as he was keeping proved a liability. Ironically, it was because he was fluent in Greek, talking with working-class people, that the right-wing authorities suspected him of communist sympathies and grew suspicious. In 1946, in Kavalla, he wrote later, 'there was a terrific to-do, knives and carbines and all the rest—and that's the origin of my getting my pension… I wasn't shot. I missed it narrowly.' He was back in Scotland soon after this, and the long-term effects of the war were only beginning to take their toll.

For Hay, the idea of Dead Ground in North Africa was matched by the living terrain at Tarbert and Argyll, its forests and fishing, that he knew so well. His experience was consolidated in the poetry that followed, some of it written very quickly and brilliantly in the war's immediate aftermath, like 'Seeker, Reaper', a breathless, unstoppable celebration of a motor fishing boat in a state of constant action and the crew in their exercise of expertise.

> When my gunnel's worn wi' raspin' nets,
> and my sides are white wi salt,
> when my ropes unlay wi haulin'
> and my steerin's aa at fault;
> when my seams are chinked and strakes are crushed,
> and the decks are tramped tae spales,
> when the length o me is sterted
> wi hammerin intae gales,
> when my motor scarce can drive me
> from off some loud sea-shore,
> then anchor me in Tarbert,
> gie me chain. And no afore.

Aa the points o Scotland
 Wi their wheelin' lights in turn
I've raised them bright ahead,
 and I've sunk them fast astern,
scourin' by the heidlands
 where new lights burn.

Despite his hospitalisation and increasing exhaustion, Hay's poems of this period are a reclamation and re-enactment of the energies of youthful appetite.

Hay's father, John Macdougall Hay, set a literary precedent with his novel *Gillespie* (1914), a dark and violent depiction of a fishing village like Tarbert devastated by the monomaniacal greed of the title character. One of its most vivid scenes is the burning of the fishing fleet in the town harbour, which may have haunted his son's vision thirty years later: 'It had a rhythmic movement which fascinated the eye. Its flat, jagged head oscillated backwards and forwards slowly, like the head of a snake. This was the main sheet of flame, whose splendour and terror mesmerised. It took a hundred fantastic shapes […] In greater gusts of the wind the wall swayed, bellied and broke, and great golden balloons hovered in the air.' But Hay senior's poetry of the First World War set a precedent for his son as well. If George Campbell Hay's poetry would be intrinsically modern and forward-looking, his father's poem 'The Call' seems prophetic:

Do not think of them as soldiers as they pass by, the
 companions of horses, living among steel and explosives.
They were men like you.
They had their own burdens, anxieties and cares;
A mother to support; children the leaving of whom behind was
 the first death.
To none is home dearer than to those who go forth to fight for
 home.
They left that sanctuary behind.

Never was war more merciless than then; never were they braver
                    than in that hour of renunciation.
They, too, had heavy thoughts as they drilled and entrenched.
They did not put off humanity when they put on a uniform.
They could weep, too.
They also had bad news in letters, and cried at nights in their
                    dug-out or billet—those devoted lads.

Perhaps this sense of human struggle, the pathos of the epic effort, to
reach across the silencing and polarising priorities of war, was what Hay
understood most terribly in the destruction of Bizerta, in Tunisia, and
it matched in his vision the burning of blitzed Clydebank and proph-
esied the deracination of Gaelic Argyll.

C'ainm a-nochd a th' orra,
na sraidean bochda anns an sgeith gach uinneag
a lasraichean 's a deatach,
a sradagan is sgreadail a luchd thuinidh,
is taigh air thaigh ga reubadh
am brionn a-cheile am bruchdadh toit a' tuiteam?
Is co a-nochd tha 'g attach
am Bas a theachd gu grad 'nan caintibh uile,
no a' spairn measg chlach is shailthean
air bhainidh a' gairm air cobhair, is nach cluinnear?
Co a-nochd a phaigheas
seann chis abhaisteach na fala cumant?

What is their name tonight,
the poor streets where every window spews
its flame and smoke,
its sparks and the screaming of its inmates,
while house upon house is rent
and collapses in a gust of smoke?
And who tonight are beseeching

Death to come quickly in all their tongues,
or are struggling among stones and beams,
crying in frenzy for help, and are not heard?

In Africa, Hay understood in the Arab world a world to balance that
of his native Gaelic Scotland, not opposed to it. The complex, multiple, partial, complementarity of cultures and languages he experienced
in Italy and Greece, confirmed this understanding. When he returned
from the war, he tried to recapture in his poetry the qualities of speed,
authenticity of engagement and immediate experience he had known
before the war. But the devastation of the war left him shattered, living
reclusively in Edinburgh, sometimes in conditions of mental distur-
bance. We would call it post-traumatic stress disorder, the long-term
result of the Dead Ground his mind had to cope with, decades after the
experience of North Africa, Italy and Greece.

Only after meeting Derick Thomson in 1978 did he reveal the long
poem he had begun decades before, allowing Thomson to publish
what there was of it in 1982. His poems and songs, now collected and
thoroughly edited with scholarly annotation by Michel Byrne, constitute a major body of work, still not fully assimilated into the history
of modern poetry. Byrne describes one of the essential themes of
'Mokhtar and Dougall' as 'the pursuit of new horizons, physical and
metaphysical.' Ahmed sets out to oppose the colonial oppressor; Omar
for adventure; Obayd searches for spiritual truth; their descendant
Mokhtar is driven towards 'the mouth of the mortar' and the silence of
what becomes literally his own Dead Ground, as it is that of his dead
companion, Dougall. In his poems, in Byrne's memorable phrase, we
have 'the harshest indictment of war by any Scottish poet.'

In 'Esta Selva Selvaggia / This Savage Wood' Hay wrote:

> Today's no ground to stand upon—
> unstable fiction balanced on
> to-morrow and the day that's gone;
> the hair of midnight, finely drawn
> between last evening and the dawn.

He brings his whole experience of 'Dead Ground' in Scotland and Africa together:

> The swaying landmines lingering down
> between Duntocher and the moon
> made Scotand and the world one.
> At last we found a civilization
> common to Europe and our nation,
> sirens, blast, disintegration.

The poem ends:

> We, having seen our yesterday,
> blasted away, explained away,
> in darkness, having no to-day,
> guess at to-morrow dawning grey,
> tighten our packstraps for the way.

Hay was a witness, an observer, and distanced in the end from any opposition, either to the vaunted 'greatness' of Britain or the clear depradations of Nazism, but seeing so clearly, in horror and sympathy, humanity's responsibility at the heart of it all. Towards the end of 'An Lagan' / 'The Hollow' he asks, 'Where are there green waves of purer foam?' and answers:

Whatever the coast they break on,
Their chill whiteness is corrupted
Even to-day, as, sparkling,
They send the pitiful dead to the land.

This reflects not only upon the Dead Ground of North Africa, of the
Second World War and all wars, but also upon the cultural identity and
language of the Gaelic world, in which even Hay's intrinsic optimism
and faith in regeneration ultimately could not rest easy or secure. The
battle continues.

Fiona Stafford

Home Front

1940. Xmas. Wednesday. 2nd Xmas of War.

Dec 31. Peter's Birthday – sent telegram & cheque. Old Year's Night very quiet only Dorf & Lew came in for a few minutes. J.B. rang up 12.15. First Old Year's Night without E & B. B.

January 1941

1 **Wednesday. New Year's Day.** *Chambers order. Arrange about Ration Books*

2 **Thursday.** *Plumbers in. Deep snow and cold*

3 **Friday.** *Very cold and snowy. Plumbers still in. Sent parcel off for Margery. Delivery of Coal. Ring up Bradley about Pot. Write to M & C. Telephone Margery, poor, could scarcely hear*

4 **Saturday.** *Very cold. Snow. Quiet night. Incendiary Bombs. Write letters to Bertha, E. Wilson, Mrs Herrick, Alice. Post letters to M&C*

5 **Sunday.** *Cold – Snow – Thaw – Frost – Quiet Night. J. B. to London. Post Letters*

6 **Monday. (Epiphany).** *Bank Cheque (B & Mckays) Ration Books (Chambers)*

7 **Tuesday.** *Miss Potts no real wool. Guys change cosy for Tracy. Pay day 9/6-*

8 **Wednesday.** *Roads dirty – snow not all gone. Chambers Ration Cards. Order – Pettit's Ration Cards. Tate's order. Dairy Order + Cream? Bank cheque (rents)*

THE DIARY, produced by T. J. and J. Smith of Clerkenwell Road, had cost three shillings and nine pence. If Mary had wanted to pay more, she could have ordered the version with a blotter, or, grander still, a volume bound in Red Glazed Basil. She opted instead for this plain, hard-wearing, page-a-day diary on utility paper, with narrow feint lines. Its brightly coloured binding, somewhere between fresh strawberry and field poppy, meant that it was unlikely to be mistaken or mislaid.

This diary had everything she required and more: the 'Calendar for 1941' offered just enough room for inserting family birthdays, before the lists and lists of Fixed and Movable Feasts, Quarter days, Bank Holidays, University Terms, Law Sittings and Changes of the Moon. More useful was the 'Postal Information', showing that a letter to H. M. Forces and Ships Abroad cost less than those to inland destinations, while the most economical communication of all was a Picture Postcard, with 'five words of greeting' permitted for the price of a penny. With the family scattered so far and wide, the official warning on this page was bleak: 'Owing to the War many Post Office Services may be suspended or modified'.

The inclusion of a small calendar for 1942 was a more encouraging augury, which, as it turned out, served Mary well, since there would be no new diary next year and the lower half of the pages in the scarlet volume purchased in December 1940 for noting engagements, records and plans in the year ahead, would eventually be reused in 1943. As a result, two years of Mary Thickett's life are still visible in tandem, with the ghost of an absent year hovering over the thin dividing line. Both years were spent in Grimsby, with occasional visits to the nearby homes of her younger twin daughters, Dorothea at Bradley and Constance in Brigg. Mary was also looking after the home of her eldest daughter, Margery, who was currently moving from camp to camp with her husband, Peter, and two children. Peter had joined the East Yorkshire Regiment soon after the War started and since then, he had been posted frequently and was now in the South West.

The early months of 1941 brought snow, ice, fog, frost and the Luftwaffe. At the head of the page for 15 January, 1941, in Mary's diary is a small diagonal cross with four dots, a mark that re-appears, with increasing frequency, from February to May. On this first, crossed day of January, Mary recorded the birthday of one of her grandchildren, a grocery order from Chambers, tea with Mrs Atkinson, a phone call from Margery, and finally, 'Siren and Gun Firing'. As the weeks pass, the dot-and-cross-lines become only too easy to decipher as the sign of an air raid. 5 February is double-crossed, beginning, '*Extremely cold, sleet, snow on ground*' and ending, '*1ˢᵗ Siren 6 o'clock. All Clear 6.30. 2ⁿᵈ 6.30 to 10*'. There were days when the alarm lasted only an hour, but there were those, like Valentine's Day, when the sirens began to hoot at 7.15 and it was not until 1.15 am that the steady sound of the 'All Clear' allowed people to emerge from their shelters and see whether their homes were still there. Sometimes Grimsby was the target; often it was merely the last town on which German planes, returning from raids on Sheffield or Leeds, could drop their surplus bombs before heading back across the North Sea.

One of the first casualties was the Municipal Library, reduced to rubble in February, 1941. Mary's diary includes the word '*Library*' on 1 March and, three weeks later, '*Library to charge*'—or perhaps '*change*'. Books are a recurring concern, featuring in lists of intent and achievement ('*Books to read*' or '*Books Read*'), and in those devoted to gifts sent and received. *Busman's Honeymoon*, the last of Dorothy Sayers' detective series, had been published in 1937. As Mary read the book during long hours spent sheltering underground as the bombs fell, she could see in Lord Peter Wimsey something of Margery's Peter, who was still suffering bouts of recurrent shellshock, as he had since the Great War. If she wondered about the effects of the current conflict, such thoughts were soon brushed away. It was difficult to think much beyond the immediate moment.

Mary's own husband William—or 'W. H. T.' as he is in the diary—was already past the age for active service in 1914. By 1940, he had been building boats in Grimsby for over half a century. As the proud fishing port's distinct identity became submerged in its newly vulnerable designation as an 'East Coast Town', W. H. T. began constructing a series of semi-subterranean shelters for Mary and each of their girls. Their only son, Harry, had served in the Royal Flying Corps during the Great War and, though injured, survived with a sense of thrilling invincibility until 1924, when he was killed in a motorcycle accident a few miles from home. W. H. T. would do everything he could to safeguard his remaining family from the danger now threatening the entire nation.

Most of the neighbours had to walk through frost and snow to the Anderson shelters at the end of the garden, built according to the standard guidelines on *Air Raid Precautions* issued by the Home Office in February 1939, when War with Germany seemed unavoidable. The steel framework, corrugated iron façade, nuts, bolts and specially designed spanner arrived as a kit for people to install, once they had excavated a large enough hole at sufficient distance from the house. Anderson shelters offered protection from explosions and falling debris, but even three feet of covering earth would not save the underlying lives from a bomb landing directly overhead.

The Thicketts descended a small flight of steps leading from the scullery and entered their underground sanctuary through a zig-zag blast wall. Their shelter stretched out between the vegetable patch and the herbaceous border, like a compact, modern, long barrow. The curved steel roof, shouldering three feet of reinforced concrete, was specifically designed to withstand a direct hit. If the house were bombed and the stairs destroyed, the four circular air holes, with their beautifully turned wooden plugs, would allow those buried inside a breathing space until the rescue team arrived. Or so the theory went. In practice, W. H. T. rarely went through the door into the dark, because, as an Air Raid Warden, he spent most of his nights on patrol or in the Wardens' Headquarters.

Mary boarded up the windows of their home every night and, when the alarms sounded, she would gather herself together with any visiting family, collecting their blue leather-cased gas masks and siren suits, before going down into the shelter to sit underground and wait. Often Mary, now seventy-three years old, spent many hours alone, underground, with only a book and her thoughts for company. As she waited

below the ground, wrapped in blankets, on a level with the root vegeta-
bles and the rabbits and the few remaining spring bulbs, her mind must
often have wandered a few hundred yards to where Harry lay buried
in the Scartho Road Cemetery. It was difficult to see ahead, impossible to sleep, during these unquiet nights. Explosions were audible
even through the snow-covered, concrete roof. The German bombers
growled in a tone quite different from the Lancasters.

On 18 February, 1941, Mary recorded '*Bombs 7 o'clock Morning.
Immingham and Waltham*'. The dawn raid targeted the Naval base in
the Humber estuary and the Wellington bombers at RAF Grimsby.
That afternoon, Margery telephoned from Cornwall to say that she
and little Gill would be arriving in two days' time. It would be a long,
complicated journey for a mother and child, on trains full of soldiers,
on tracks vulnerable to attack.

As the raids and anxieties intensified, so did Mary's preparations—
there were bedrooms to be cleaned, extra ingredients to be ordered,
though the diary records her frustration: '*no currants*', '*no Atora suet*' and
only '*tinned milk*'. The wool fund run by the Presbyterian Church got a
donation nevertheless. Margery and Gill's arrival was marked by '*More
Bread. Plum Loaves. Cakes. More milk. Boiled Chicken*' and followed by
a week of tea parties and family visits, all fitted around Mary's work
at the Hospital. On 27 February, Mary managed to squeeze in a Hair
appointment at 11.30, after the Bring and Buy sale at Springfield, but
the rest of the day was punctuated by a siren at 1.20 and another at 5
o'clock. The final line reads '*9 Persons killed—Oberon, Cleethorpe Rd,
top of Freeman Street.*'

In fact the number of casualties was higher. The bar at the Oberon
Pub had been full of regulars—off-duty servicemen keeping their spirits
buoyant until the next call to Action Stations; dockers who worked all
hours to maintain the ships and operate the locks; trawler-men who
scaled the cliff-like breakers of the North Sea, navigated mines and
sustained aerial attacks, in order to haul in fish for a besieged nation.
A single Dornier strafed the local school before riddling the road with
machine gun fire and dropping its bombs. A nine year old girl was

buying carrots when the greengrocer's shop shattered over her. Dozens more were injured as the buildings broke all around.

The almost daily sirens continued; the taping of windows; the drawing of black-out curtains; the descents into the dark ground; the brief records in Mary's diary: '*Planes overhead. Gunfire*'. Life was carrying on in its peculiar way. Two weeks after the Oberon bombing, Mary arranged an early hair appointment because she was going to spend the day with Constance. Things did not go quite as hoped, as the summary jotted down later that day reveals in its stark concision: '*Brigg—Puncture—Walk. Lift by R. Davis. Bus to Grimsby. Home 8.40. Siren 8.45.*' The most surprising detail is the final note, presumably added the following day: '*Calm sleep.*'

Where unmarked by dots and crosses, Mary's pages usually begin with the words '*All Clear*' or '*Quiet Night.*' On 8 May, the cross is followed by '*Bad night.*' This almost certainly refers to the Hull Blitz. Already, during April, Hull had suffered multiple fatalities even among those in air raid shelters, because of the sustained bombardment. On 8 May, the attacks reached a peak of intensity and hundreds of civilians were killed in the raid on the City Square. Those in Grimsby, across the gaping black mouth of the Humber Estuary, saw the night lighting up with unnatural flares and flashes. The sky glowed for days and nights, with a dull, relentless blaze.

If Mary's nights were disrupted by sirens and descents into the air-raid shelter, her days were devoted to maintaining order. Meticulous accounts, regular appointments, lists of groceries and records of correspondence are interspersed with a highly organised programme of cleaning: '**3 March.** *Wash Day. Cupboards in Bathroom.* **4 March.** *Pantry cupboards. Dressing Room cleaned.* **5 March.** *Clean Cupboards.* **6 March.** *Finish Pantry Cupboards. Finish Bathroom Cupboards.* **10 March.** *Clean Top Rooms.* **19 March.** *Clean Drawing Room. Box Room. Linen Cupboard.* **20 March.** *Plumbers in Back Laundry.* **21 March.** *Bathroom and Laundry Finished.* **26 March.** *China Cupboard cleaned.* **27 March.** *Dining Room (cleaned).* **3 April.** *Clean silver from upstairs. Do cupboards.*' The more insistent the sirens, the more rubble-strewn the streets, the shabbier the exterior of every house, the more immaculate Mary's interior became.

If it were not for the dots, crosses and notes on the precise timing of the raids, there were days which might now be mistaken for ordinary existence. There were others on which personal and cosmic disorder seemed to have conspired together. Mary was born in the same year as the Queen Mother, whose birthday was one of the few dates printed in the diary. In 1941, the day also marked a critical moment for the British Navy, with news of the disastrous sinking of H. M. S. Hood, followed by the rapid pursuit of the Bismarck, as Mary recorded, among other matters:

> **Monday 26 May (Mary the Queen Mother born, 1867)**
> *Quiet Night. See Burkett. Settled Account. Chemist. Yeast. / Hood, British Warship sunk by Germans*
>
> **Tuesday 27 May** *Quiet Night. Tate's Account paid. Order (very little). Chamber's Order, Fish, Cod & Kippers. Margery Dentist (5.30). German Bismarck warship sunk by British.*

If the domestic detail here seems dwarfed by the Battle of the Atlantic, a few days later it begins to loom very much larger as a further appointment, '*Margery Dentist 1pm*', is followed by the words '*17 teeth*'. Mary's tentative note on Thursday, 29 May - '*Horlicks? Rice Puddings?*' - takes on new meaning in this unhappy sequence. Margery stayed on for a fortnight, convalescing after this extraordinary extraction, but by 16 June, their correspondence resumes, with Mary now despatching letters to Bideford in North Devon.

Still the pages were crossed with air raid signs, but the weather at least was kinder. Sunday 29 June 1941 begins '*Siren 2.45*', before turning into '*Beautiful Day. Hot.*' The end of June brought a '*Lovely Day*' spent brushing down the outdoor cushions and furniture and '*Gardening with Ethel.*' A week of quiet nights prompted fewer notes in the diary and even when the raids began again, the pages are generally emptier. On Wednesday, 23 July, the only activity recorded is '*Tennis. 8. Dorothea.*'

After that, there is nothing until 1 November. It seems that the scarlet diary was lost after all. Perhaps it lay forgotten in the tennis pavilion, perhaps buried in the grandest air raid shelter of all, beneath the garden at Bradley. Mary must have retrieved her book in time for the Christmas preparations, for the final weeks of the year are packed with recipes, accounts, and lists of guests and presents, as if making up for the blankness of late summer. 1942 passed unrecorded, or noted down in the pages of a diary now lost. For in January 1943, Mary picked up her old, red volume and began another year.

The brevity of the entries for 1943, written in a slightly less steady hand, show that the intervening year had taken its toll. Mary, now seventy-five, started the annual record on January 6, 1943, apparently prompted by the weather: '*Snow & Sleet.*' The next day brought only '*Rheumatism in Knee—Lumbago also,*' followed by two days '*In bed.*' On Monday, 11 January, Mary had to send apologies for absence from the Monthly Meeting of the Nurses Institution. In some respects, things were not greatly changed: Saturday, 18 January, 1941, had seen '*Meat difficult—no pork or sausages. Butter 1/7 pound. Ration for 3, 6 ounces*'; lower down the page, the entry for the equivalent Saturday in 1943 reads, '*Meat rationed Fowls. G. Fowl. Pheasant... Burkitt's order - Boiling Fowl.*' But between the rationing record and the butcher's order is a fainter note, more difficult to decipher: '*Treatment 10 o'clock.*'

Mary's appetite for reading was as keen as ever. On 30 January, she listed several classics, '*Tristram Shandy. History of Mr Polly, H. G. Wells. Cricket and the Hearth, C. Reade*', together with a new title: '*We Landed at Dawn*'. The War correspondent, Alexander Berry Austin, had been quick to turn his despatches into a book, but perhaps in the lost pages of 1942, Mary had already noted the disastrous dawn raid on Dieppe. The blank weeks of late summer and autumn 1941, when her diary had been left untouched, were now being put to service for new resolutions. Jotted onto the page for 1ˢᵗ August, 1941, is a note from *The Sunday Times* review section for 21 March 1943: '*Books to read. The Last of Summer, Kate o'Brien, The Heart is a Lonely Hunter, C. McCullers, Concertina Farm, Erick Berry & Herbert Best.*' *Concertina Farm* had been reviewed somewhat ambivalently by H. E. Bates, who regarded the cheerfully escapist account of keeping hens at a summer retreat in the Adirondacks as both a damning commentary on 'our modern civilisation' and 'a whiff of smelling-salts in a fainting world'. This may have been just what Mary Thickett needed in 1943.

In the early months of the year, Mary's diary includes regular references to Sirens, settling bills, letters, lunches, library books, coupons and cleaning, interspersed with less routine details such as the entry for 31 March '*Women's Luncheon Club - Speaker on Russia*', '*Summer Lighting*' on 4 April, or the draft of an advertisement, '*Nurses Ages 17 to 60, must register—anyone with training—Male or Female Midwifes. Student Nurses. V. A. D.*' What becomes a very regular entry in the spring of 1943, in fainter and fainter writing, is the single word, 'Treatment.' On Easter Sunday, Mary's plans for the family lunch were in some doubt, judging by the question mark: '*Meal? Boiled Fowl. Salads—Mixed Veg—Beetroot—sweets.*' There are no entries at all for the days following, but on Thursday 29 April, 1943, a note in Margery's hand states that '*Mother died.*'

Reports in the Grimsby papers on 30 April show the widespread shock over Mary's death, which was entirely unexpected even by her husband, W. H. T. 'Yesterday morning Mrs Thickett appeared to be quite well at breakfast time', reported the *Grimsby News*. The notice describes her tireless work as the President and wartime Chair of the Nursing Institution, her contributions to the Hospital Ladies Linen Guild and the Grimsby Education Committee, acknowledging at length that 'very few social or charitable movements in Grimsby failed to receive her help'.

A week later, the Grimsby Electricity Committee made their public tribute, describing Mrs Thickett as 'a wonderful wife and helpmate' and 'a model mother to her children and grandchildren', before concluding that 'she was a staunch and sympathetic friend to everyone, and that the town had suffered a great loss by her passing'. Mary's funeral took place in St James's Church on Wednesday 5 May, 1943. She was buried with Harry in the south borders of the Scartho Road Cemetery, her name carved into the same grey gravestone.

Mary did not live to see the bomb that destroyed the North Transept of St James's three months later, nor the hard rain of butterfly bombs. Grimsby had the unlucky distinction of being one of only a handful of British towns to be subjected to these deadly devices, designed to resemble tins of food and, when dropped randomly over people weakened by shortages, intended to cause maximum destruction to civilians. When touched, the cylindrical bombs opened out, as if spreading wings, and exploded. The months after Mary's death saw huge warning posters pasted everywhere and painstaking searches of Grimsby's lofts, garages, parks and gardens, where innocent shrubs or spreading rhubarb leaves were concealing lethal weapons with pastoral names. Even years after the War, unsuspecting dogs rootling in undergrowth were still occasionally blown to pieces.

Mary died without knowing whether the German or Allied Forces would eventually prevail, or how many more years the War would last, or whether any of her family and friends would be left alive at the end of it. In the event, all of her grandchildren survived to have children and grandchildren of their own. Mary's diary, carefully preserved by Margery, who gave it a title, *The Last Diary of Mary Thickett—1941–April 1943*, remains in family hands.

Alice Spawls

Paul Nash's Land Unfit for Humans

PAUL NASH was born in May 1889, during the twilight of the Victorians. His father William was a barrister, and the three Nash children—Paul the eldest, his brother John and sister Barbara—grew up at Iver Heath, in spacious, ordered Buckinghamshire countryside. The landscape beyond their garden was one of cornfields and copses, elms, pines and water-drenched alder carrs. Nash realised at a young age that there was 'some trouble haunting our home. Often mother seemed disinclined to eat.' Caroline Nash was subject to depressions, and other, stronger incapacitations that saw her spend long periods in nursing homes and psychiatric wards. Paul himself was physically fragile and ill at ease in the world, seeking out intense relationships with certain spots where he was free from adult supervision: the garden at Iver Heath and a shady part of Kensington Gardens (which he called 'my first authentic place'), among others.

He studied first at Chelsea Polytechnic and in 1908, the year of his first 'nocturnal visions', he moved to the London County Council School of Photo-Engraving and Lithography, just off Fleet Street. 'The whole place,' he wrote, 'had an atmosphere of liveliness and work.' The students were learning art as a living, preparing to become efficient producers of 'posters, show cards, layouts and other more or less remunerative designs'. Nash fell for the Pre-Raphaelites, then for Blake and Samuel Palmer. His drawings of trees and quiet landscapes caught the attention of William Rothenstein, who became his first supporter and suggested Nash consider the Slade. He arrived in 1910 with the now famous generation that included Stanley Spencer, Mark Gertler, David Bomberg, C. R. W. Nevinson and Dora Carrington, but Henry

Tonks, the hard-to-please drawing master, dismissed his sketches on arrival. 'It was evident he considered that neither the Slade, nor I, was likely to derive much benefit,' Nash later said. He left within a year, and thought of it after as a 'barren' time. Iver Heath, where his brother John was painting the landscapes and scenes that also animated Paul, was a more attractive prospect than Tonks's studio, though it meant leaving behind his fellow students on the cusp of a modernist moment.

Nash looked backwards rather than forwards, to the great English landscape watercolourists—John Sell Cotman, Thomas Girtin and John Crome—and made a series of tree studies: he was especially fond of Wittenham Clumps, a pair of wooded hills near his uncle's home in Berkshire. It became one of the talismanic places he depicted again and again. These early landscapes, languid and pale, show Nash's limitations, as well as his early (and life-long) inspirations; they give little suggestion of what would come next. In 1914 he joined the Artists' Rifles and went to the front in 1916, though he was sent back with an injured rib before seeing action. Nonetheless the drawings he had made there brought him a commission as an official war artist, like his brother John. He returned to a very different war, at Ypres Salient, depicting the aftermath of the Battle of Passchendaele, and was almost immediately exposed to a poison gas attack. 'I am no longer an artist,' he wrote in a (now notorious) letter; 'I am a messenger to those who want the war to go on for ever ... may it burn their lousy souls.' He came under frequent shellfire and described the experience as 'unspeakable, godless, hopeless ... sunset and sunrise are blasphemous, they are mockeries to man.'

This marked the end of Nash's gothic romanticism of place, and the beginning of his representations of a brutalised world. It was the decline, he wrote, of 'the human element' as men 'became monsters' and 'machines, pictorially speaking, took the place of men.' Later war artists such as Eric Ravilious chose to give centre stage to the instruments of war, but nearly always in a benign, off-duty moment; the planes and ships strangely humanised. Nash's drawings and watercolours from the trenches show landscapes where the human is a pitiful or impossible sight, and technology is seen in all its violence. In 'The Landscape, Hill', Nash's earlier greens and browns are dulled to dun and grey; the yellow is chemical, the sky full of unnatural bursts of black smoke and falling shrapnel. The Palmer-inspired hillocks and hedges of his previous work transform into the clefts and ridges of earth mutilated by destructive processes. The tropes of Nash's First World War sketches are broken trees, riven ground, dark pools of water, rain which falls from the air like spears, searchlights in the dark, barbed wire. His compositions took on a new dynamism; the previously awkward middle ground now shaped by the unnatural furrows of the trenches, the props and detritus of mechanised battle.

Nash had been trained in military cartography, the knack, as Henry Reed describes it in 'Judging Distances', of 'how to report on a landscape'. This was not the sort of 'reporting' Nash had done before, where reality and imagination were allowed to gently inflect each other. In fact, this skill required a reconceptualisation of the land for an artist who was already so preoccupied by it. Partly this was a question of space—'judging distances'—and partly one of detachment: a field was no longer a field, a barn no longer a barn. Nash's looking was now in the service of far from Romantic causes and the new field was a gridded one, a killing zone. His training in maps, ironically, altered his compositional process. He began to lay out the features of the landscape, including trees, geometrically (as in his most famous interwar painting, 'Wood on the Downs'). His barbed wire entanglements show a professional familiarity.

In the trenches Nash could only do quick work—sketches and watercolours. When he returned home he painted in oil for the first time: dense, crowded and distinctly ungraceful images of a churned and ravaged landscape, where, especially in the bitterly titled 'We Are Making a New World', the sun rises innocently (the long white beams bisect the canvas) on scenes of complete devastation. In oils Nash seemed very quickly to have surmounted his earlier painterly difficulties, using the heft of the paint to shape the churned-up earth. In 'The Ypres Salient at Night', the 'weird greenish glare' of the searchlights illuminates metal, water, bunkers and wire to make a ghostly pattern across the landscape. This is land unfit for humans, land which they enter at great peril.

These new canvases were larger than anything Nash had worked on before; 'The Menin Road', in particular, covers a wall and looks almost like a tapestry in its dense and detailed arrangement, and its flattened areas of colour. Here the broken trees jut up like gnarled totem poles, a mockery of a forest, and the two small figures urgently crossing the ground seem pitifully exposed. It's hard to imagine a place one would less like to be. The annihilation of the earth—there is nothing green in sight—seems to herald the end of days, a horror from which there is no return. The burnt-out plants look like bones, the ruptured pieces of machinery are warped and rusted, the one tree-like shape is really a cloud of orange smoke, and the blue light that breaks through the dark and heavy clouds is not that of a hopeful morning but searchlights which the retreating soldiers must run from. The ground is divided by jagged incursions of water—not the natural curves of rivers—and the reflections of the broken trees in the water look mechanistic, cruel and metallic.

Nash's war paintings were exhibited at the 'Void of War' exhibition in 1918 and brought him sudden acclaim. Arnold Bennett wrote that they seemed 'to have been done in a kind of rational and dignified rage'; Herbert Read praised him for capturing 'the phantasmagoric atmosphere of No Man's Land'. But, as Nash later put it, he was now 'a war artist without a war'. His health was shaky, he suffered from nightmares and his certainty wavered. In the interwar period Nash positioned himself at the forefront of English debates about artistic Modernism, always arguing from and for his dual position, trying to reconcile 'internationalism versus an indigenous culture; renovation versus conservatism; the industrial versus the pastoral; the functional versus the futile.'

His own work was closer to Surrealism—he wasn't socially radical in his work, and in both theme and style he drifted from the stark war palette back to a muted pastoral. But the allure of place had been compromised by war, or rather, war had given the land a new agency: one that could be fearful and hostile to humans. De Chirico, whose paintings always seem to have their own mysterious logic, was an important discovery, and the destabilised architecture of Nash's inter-war paintings suggests an artist who needed to disrupt, not out of anarchic tendencies but because, as Louis MacNeice wrote, 'world is crazier and more of it than we think.' Nash suffered from 'black-outs', collapses common to many victims of post-traumatic stress, the first of which occurred in 1921, while he was living on the South Coast, and led to a remarkable series of sea pictures—clean and bleak and cold and ordered. The nerve specialist Gordon Holmes recognised the familiar symptom of intrusive memories from the front, a 'continuous series of frightening images'.

The war didn't however ruin Nash's belief in a progressive human rela-tionship to the landscape; indeed the currents of European Modernism seemed to encourage a post-pastoral sensibility in his work, despite the horrors of war. One of his photographs from the period shows two friends performing salutations in front of a pylon; the interwar decades were a time of sudden change in the countryside, with cars altering both the countryside's appearance and accessibility (one critic thanked Nash for reminding him that roads and pylons could be attractive).

Nash at times seems obstinately avant-garde: though he was greatly interested in prehistoric art, he claimed that the Huffington chalk horse wasn't important as a historic masterwork but for the opportunity it afforded to experience a site where 'the landscape asserts itself with all the force of its triumphant fusion of natural and artificial design.' In photographs of the spot he deliberately distorts and flattens the perspective, obscuring the design so that the lines of white chalk appear to divide the dark hill arbitrarily.

In an essay on 'Unseen Landscapes' for *Country Life* he wrote that his preferred landscapes 'are not part of the unseen world in the psychic sense, nor are they part of the unconscious, they belong to the world that lies, visibly, about us … all these things under consideration here—stones, bones, empty fields, demolished houses and back gardens—all these have their trivial feature, as it were their blind side, but, also, they have another character.' Nash had always believed in the mystical potential of landscape and increasingly this manifested in attempts to invest his landscapes with a reality unknowable to humans, or at least a character more terrifying and independent than the genre usually acknowledged.

One of his obsessions was a series of fallen trees, which he both photographed and painted as he sought to capture their particular strangeness. 'If they had been no more than trees in their perpendicular life it was as much as you could believe,' he wrote. 'Horizontally they had assumed or acquired the personality of monsters.' Nash brought a similar attitude to group of watercolours of crashed German planes, which he thought of not as the inanimate detritus of past conflict but having 'diverse, distinct personalities'. He was attracted, he said, to the object (organic or not) out of its natural element, and the way in which this displacement created the 'monstrous' in the landscape.

These ideas continued into his World War Two paintings. When war broke out, Nash found himself a war artist for the second time, attached to the Air Ministry, which presumably delighted him (he loved flight in all its forms). His anthropomorphic images of aeroplanes upset officials and they ended his contract after a year, but Kenneth Clark intervened, insisting that the War Artists' Advisory Committee put aside the substantial sum of £500 to buy paintings of aerial conflict from Nash, which gave him almost complete freedom. He returned to larger canvases again; the results were as striking as his First World War paintings and include three of his best works: 'Totes Meer', 'The Battle of Britain' and 'The Battle of Germany'.

'Totes Meer' was inspired by the metal recovery unit at Cowley, near the home in Oxford he and his wife Margaret had moved to in 1939. Nash took a number of photographs and made sketches of wrecked Luftwaffe planes at the site, then composed the jagged metal parts into an image of a great frozen sea, which crashes onto the foreground plain. The wounds inflicted on the land are painted as great gashes. Yet in the distance the Palmer moon—that quaint pastoral moon—still hangs;

beyond this metal sea is a sliver of fields and horizon that seems to offer salvation, if one can get to the other side.

'The Battle of Britain' imagines the aerial contest as seen looking down over an English estuary: the great swirls of white smoke create graceful, almost organic patterns around the passing clouds—they could be the motions of swifts in flight, a dancer, or flowers unfurling—but here and there are vertical tails of black as a pilot crashes down, and in the distance faint, ordered marks signify ranks of oncoming squadrons. The spectator is set high above the land; the view down onto the serpentine river recalls Turner's 'View along the Valley of a River', but also puts one in the position of an approaching bomber pilot (a position Nash would have liked to be in himself).

The light and fluid paintwork in the foreground is some of Nash's best, and the incongruous beauty of the spectacle, which seems to exult in the greater power of nature (as ordering principle, as the inevitability of death, as regeneration)—a very different sentiment from his First World War paintings—prompted Clark to write to Nash: 'I think in this and 'Totes Meer' you have discovered a new form of allegorical painting. It is impossible to paint great events without allegory … and you have discovered a way of making the symbols out of the events themselves.' Perhaps it helped that he was commemorating a British victory, and that the horror of war was not experienced first-hand this time.

Nash's final painting for the WAAC, 'The Battle of Germany', is even more unconventional. Painted as the Allies were invading Germany, it shows a great mass of smoke rising over the horizon. The sky is turned half red by the blaze; the city in the foreground is cast under the shadow of the smoke. The left-hand side shows—in Nash's words—'the suspense of the waiting city under the quiet though baleful moon' (the moon is tinged with red) while the other side shows the city already under bombardment, with smaller explosions thrown up in the middle distance. What strikes one most of all, however, is the near abstraction of the image into a chromatic field, almost a patchwork (it's reminiscent of patterns and textiles of the period).

As Clark suggested, the painting represents one direction Nash might have taken after the war; as it was he died the following year. The expressive, colourist landscapes he painted in 1946, including a group of paintings of Wittenham Clumps, one of his first mystic places, are alien but without the suggestion of human violence. The land is broken up in the manner of Cézanne—painted in small coloured areas, each with its own velocity—and the tones are warm and bright. These are landscapes where nature has asserted itself over humans, where there is no dead ground. The pastoral is complicated though by the strange floating presences Nash painted in the skies: a giant magnolia unfolding, a face, a huge sunflower eclipsing the sun.

Do these speak of death from the air, of bombers and zeppelins and clouds of poisonous gas? Or is Nash turning those unforgettable sights of his war days into visions of a different order, reminding us that nature is more terrifying and beautiful than anything man can make, that even the destroyed landscape of 'The Menin Road' will see days of gold and green again. We can't know for sure: he was cut off just when these post-war images were taking shape. They exist in the realm of the fantastic, and, perhaps, remind us that of all the forces beyond our control, the most dangerous is other people thinking they can shape the face of the world.

The Ypres Salient at Night, 1918. Imperial War Museum

We Are Making a New World, 1918. Imperial War Museum

The Menin Road, 1919. Imperial War Museum

The Battle of Britain, 1941. Imperial War Museum

The Battle of Germany, 1944. Imperial War Museum

John Greening

Marshland

WRITING to an eager Siegfried Sassoon in February 1918, Edmund Gosse recommended that he should 'get into friendly relations with Mr Marsh, who is a most charming man, extremely interested in poetry, and the personal friend of all the new poets'. And indeed, few poets could reach the sunlit uplands of acclaim except by way of this particular Marshland at the centre of the British establishment.

Edward Marsh was, for the better part of twenty-three years, Churchill's Private Secretary. To be within his preserve, to know 'Eddie', was to be in a charmed circle. Marsh had money behind him, the proceeds of compensation ('murder money') for the assassination of his great grandfather, Sir Spencer Perceval. With its help he brought out the immensely popular Georgian Poetry series—five hardback anthologies between 1912 and 1922 (once common in secondhand bookshops).

It is often forgotten that before the First World War, Georgian poetry was seen as radical, ground-breaking, an escape from the pre-Freudian forests of Victorian verse and the smoky dreamland of the Nineties— something clearer, more open-air, plainspoken, using a bracing everyday language. This proved just the style for war poetry (and several of Sassoon's now celebrated pieces did find their way into the 1917 and 1919 anthologies) but naturally that wasn't what Marsh had originally anticipated. As his biographer, Christopher Hassall, points out, 'With the fourth volume (1919) the very term "Georgian" came to mean something different.'

Marsh had been moved to begin his project when Rupert Brooke brought out his debut collection in 1911. Brooke was, of course, not a war poet at that stage, and he represented everything the older man admired. When the golden boy died four years later, even as sales of the anthologies and of Brooke's poetry rocketed (Marsh was his literary executor), the slow draining of the civil servant's influence had already begun.

A glance at some of the names in *Georgian Poetry 1911–1912* breeds the suspicion that he was not quite as attuned to the modern as he believed: G. K. Chesterton, T. Sturge Moore, James Stephens, James Elroy Flecker sit alongside Rupert Brooke, W. W. Gibson, and D. H. Lawrence. Reviewing this first book in the series, Lawrence (whose own 'Snap-Dragon' featured in it), compared the experience to 'a big breath taken when we are waking up after a night of oppressive dreams,' but in his correspondence with the editor, he teases him for being 'a police-man in poetry', that his ear 'has got stiff and a bit mechanical.'

The effect is perhaps best demonstrated by the case of Wilfrid Gibson, one of Marsh's main players, appearing in all five anthologies —cool, colloquial, non-metropolitan (Gibson was from Hexham), utterly un-Victorian and a best-seller in his day. By the time he died in 1962, he was remembered only for the school anthology pieces, 'Flannan Isle' and 'The Ice Cart', or perhaps for having been the first to publish Brooke's 'The Soldier'.

Nowadays as we look back a hundred years his name is apparently absent from the landscape: truly dead ground in the military sense, because he has not gone away, appearing regularly in books about Robert Frost for having failed to defend him in a fight with a game-keeper (Frost called him 'the worst snob in England)'. In fact, Gibson wrote very successfully about the war but like Brooke, he never set foot on a battlefield. He simply imagined it. Larkin said of him (even while he anthologised him): 'a lifetime of books, ending with a Macmillan's *Collected Poems* just like Yeats or Hardy or C. Rossetti. Never wrote a good poem in his life.'

It's a curious fate. The light suddenly changes, and what had for so many years appeared to be a fully achieved modern aesthetic turns out to be a facade. Camouflage was, after all, one of the essential arts of trench warfare, and Gibson did a very good job of concealing his tracks, persuading many readers (and Macmillan) that he had actually done his bit. But one has to admire a writer who could so convincingly conjure those unseen killing fields (notably in *Battle, and Other Poems* (1916)), even if he is at his most poignant when grounded on his home turf, and enriched by someone else's music. Ivor Gurney's setting of his 'Black Stitchel', for example, (from the 1918 collection, *Whin*) is unforgettable.

By the time Edward Marsh's series had caught the public's imagination, several of the poets it was introducing were struggling in a rather more literal and morbid marsh. Some reached in their poetry for radical escape routes, especially Ezra Pound's free-verse duckboards. Pound knew full well how the old guard (like his friend 'BinBin'—Laurence Binyon) clung to archaic words and values when he wrote: 'There died a myriad/And of the best, among them,/For an old bitch gone in the teeth,/For a botched civilization...' His was a narrow way; the dedicated Modernist was not encouraged to deviate, so it's not surprising that Pound, initially on the shortlist for the Georgian anthologies, soon had little time for them or their editor.

That way went Isaac Rosenberg (encouraged in fact by Marsh, who wrote to him in the trenches), showing extraordinary balance and dignity and intelligence, until he was killed in 1918; here was a truly cosmopolitan voice, free of formal fustiness, radical in tone and diction. An East Ender ('horribly rough' said Pound, who also came to appreciate him), and an essentially urban soul, Rosenberg was a gifted visual artist—as was David Jones, who had nothing at all to do with the Marsh birds—and heard an entirely different music, following the lure of his own private mythology. That way too went Richard Aldington, his gaze fixed on the Very Lights of Imagism, until he fell into biography.

The most interesting of the poets to emerge from this period, however, are those who never quite lost touch with the Georgian air, tracking its ignis fatuus but with their eyes wide open. Thus, Edward Thomas up until his death at an Observation Post in Arras, and Robert Graves right into the age of smoky television studio lights where he sat talking to Malcolm Muggeridge. Thomas (who, tellingly, was never selected for any of Marsh's books) hardly mentions the war, except in passing references or casual exchanges, as with the ploughman of 'As the Team's Head Brass', yet the depopulated landscape he evokes is clearly a war-time one. And we remember how he picked up that clod of earth to show Eleanor Farjeon what he was fighting for: 'literally, for this'. The ground was never dead to Edward Thomas.

As it happened, this was a war taking place in rural locations; it was a place where people went to walk or cycle as he had walked or cycled 'In Pursuit of Spring' or 'The South Country'. He felt no obligation to write about the Paris Metro or the smell of steaks in passageways. The bloom of dust on nettles interested him more than conventional romantic blooms. Thomas could convey the grief and longing of a nation through cherry blossom or rain or a wood-pile or falling apples or a winding footpath, and he had a real feeling for what his friend Frost called 'sentence sounds': the natural rhythms of English that seemed to have gone with the wind (or with Yeats) since the Nineties. Thus he became the war poet most contemporary British poets are likely to be influenced by, the least rhetorical, the most trusted, untainted by Marsh gas.

Graves, on the other hand, might as easily have been writing under an earlier King George: quirkier, not really a man of the earth, as unmappable as his curious poem 'Lost Acres' would suggest. He undoubtedly had an eye to the main chance (he is in three of the profitable anthologies) and was too creatively impulsive to be trusted, as Blunden and Sassoon discovered when they read his best-selling war memoir and felt obliged to annotate it with over five and a half thousand words of exasperated comment and correction. Graves suppressed most of his own war poetry, which is why we have tended to overlook its importance. It's as if when he found that his own death had been announced in the *Times* he saw it as a chance to say goodbye to all that. He became a writer of timeless love poems, and of prose whose example of clarity one wishes Edward Thomas (author of so many vaporous potboilers) had lived to follow.

Then there are those who have gradually begun to appear as the mists have cleared—notably, all the women Marsh excluded from his anthologies. Vera Brittain, Charlotte Mew, have now been fully recognised, and others such as May Wedderburn Cannan, Margaret Postgate Cole, May Sinclair received their due in the all-female *Scars Upon My Heart*; more recently, Tim Kendall's OUP anthology has drawn our attention to the extraordinary Mary Borden; and the unique genius of Hope Mirrlees's vision of post-war Paris is at last plain to see. It is understandable that women's writing from the war took longer to filter through, and that its strengths lie in individual poems rather than oeuvres but there is no excuse for Marsh's reluctance. Of the five anthologies, the first three were all male affairs; thereafter (even he could not ignore what they had contributed to the war) only Fredegond Shove and Vita Sackville-West.

One remarkable figure to step from the apparently dead ground and into the twenty-first century is Ivor Gurney, a poet much preoccupied with the particular named location, forever making connections between landscape in Gloucestershire and the Somme. It is hard to forget the image of him sheltering from the barrage at Caulaincourt while writing the poem, 'Severn Meadows', one of the few of his own he set to music. And this was something quite new, hardly known since Campion and Dowland (though we take it for granted in the Age of Dylan).

Gurney, who so loved maps, who suddenly came out of himself at Dartford Asylum when Helen Thomas (Edward's widow) produced Ordnance Surveys of the paths he knew so well, is even now redrawing the map of English poetry, and this is likely to continue with the imminent publication of a three volume Complete Poems. But at the time, he was misunderstood, not least by Marsh, who did offer help from the 'Rupert Brooke fund', yet who would never fully appreciate how the events of 1914–18 were making a new fractured style of verse the mainstream. Suddenly, T. S. Eliot's *The Waste Land* was more to the point than, say, *The End of the World* by Lascelles Abercrombie, intended to be the climax to *Georgian Poetry 1913–1915*, a volume which all but ignored the war.

Edmund Blunden's is an interesting case. In many ways he never escaped the influence of Marsh and his Georgian poets, even though he was too young to have met them before the war (he joined up straight from school at Christ's Hospital) and even though one might have expected the Somme and Passchendaele to have devastated any attractions that style might hold. He lost many of his best war poems in the poisonous mud around Ypres in 1917, but it wasn't those that Marsh would have wanted anyway for his fifth (and least successful) anthology.

It suited him that Blunden was predominantly a pastoralist, a 'harmless young shepherd in a soldier's coat'; and those pastoral conventions, as followed by the poet's beloved Collins and Clare, would not be shifted even by the harshest barrage. Robert Graves asked Marsh to take on Blunden 'as a sacred charge', and the young veteran was one of those who benefited considerably from his patron's 'Rupert money' in the years immediately after the war. The successful man of letters who lived into the 1970s was forever making himself, as he put it in his memoir, *Undertones of War*, 'go over the ground again', but never quite managing to find a way forward. It is easy for the reader to feel bogged down in Blunden's poetry (which is yet to be properly collected), but even F. R. Leavis detected that there were more interesting things going on there than in most Georgian verse.

The labyrinths and synchronicities and juxtapositions, the evocations of a Lewis Carroll world of military protocol, pointless rituals, recurring idiocies, and his many accounts of being lost on the battlefield (not to mention his dreams and ghostly encounters) are expressions of Blunden's struggle to make his poetry both adequate to the times he lives in, and an adequate memorial to the men he knew. He never comes close to winning Eliot's 'intolerable struggle' and it can seem as if he is undertaking his own 'raid on the inarticulate' with the poetic equivalent of muskets and cavalry. The long poem 'Third Ypres' is where he almost breaks free, the emotion rattling the cages of the form, and one cannot imagine the fastidious Eddie Marsh appreciating it.

The obvious name has not come up. Where does he fit into this landscape? Surely this is hallowed ground. When Craig Raine steps on to it and suggests that Wilfred Owen 'has read, quite uncritically, too much bad Keats and worse Shelley' or when C. H. Sisson, noting 'Above all I am not concerned with poetry', puts on his hobnail boots and says 'if his work is not that, it can only be some inferior form of literature'—isn't this sacrilege?

Owen's is lush green territory: the verse invites with a rich romantic density, and has terrible things to reveal. We have all been there and will not forget it in a hurry. Marsh was wary of it, however, as if he half recognised the truth in John Middleton Murry's remark that coming to Owen after one of the Georgian anthologies, 'you will not find those beautiful poems less beautiful than they are, but you will find in "Strange Meeting" an awe, an immensity, an adequacy to that which has been most profound in the experience of a generation.'

But it could be argued that Owen is dead ground for succeeding poets (such as Raine and Sisson). There is too much that is obvious, symbols, half-rhymes, poking up, and romantic iconography still haunting there. Only when we move away from the Marshland, and 'Move him into the sun', do we see the glimmerings of genius.

Now that over a century has passed since the Georgian Poetry series was launched, and the name of the man who edited them requires a footnote, we can safely assume that there is not going to be more than a local revival of interest in Lascelles Abercrombie, Gordon Bottomley, John Drinkwater, John Freeman, Harold Monro, Ralph Hodgson. Those who were likely to make their mark have done so, maybe for just one or two poems, as with John Masefield, the idiosyncratic W. H. Davies and Walter de la Mare.

Even Robert Nichols, who features several times in the books, and who might be thought to be a ripe for rediscovery, is unlikely now to make a great impression. Nichols's heroic note no longer rings true (Graves was scathing of his 'crippled warrior' performances in

America) and there is far less to recommend him to today's readers than in Wilfrid Gibson. Generations of literary critics have drained the private Marshland of Georgian England and given a new name to its dead ground. It is now clearly marked War Poetry, and it might be thought that today's poets, who have only experienced war from afar, would be excluded. Yet on the horizon, the old barbed wire silhouetted behind them, like metrical lines they have had to negotiate, they keep on coming.

There is Michael Longley, unable to forget his own father's time on the Somme, and Geoffrey Hill clutching his copy of Péguy; Andrew Motion and Glyn Maxwell are looking for Edward Thomas; John Gurney is bringing up the rear, carrying the largest pack of all, an epic poem *War* (1996), which is still out in that No Man's Land where long poems can hide for what seems like decades. And there are women, too—Carol Ann Duffy is taking a roll call, looking for new recruits. Susan Wicks, Helen Dunmore, Jenny Lewis, Patricia McCarthy … All look uncomfortable here amid the silence, except perhaps Hughes who forges ahead, stalking 'our national ghost', like that hulk imagined in Georg Trakl's great poem of 1911 (yes, there is foreign war poetry out there), 'Der Krieg':

> He's risen now, who slept so long,
> He's risen from deep vaults among
> The day's remains. Huge and unknown
> He stands. His black hands crush the moon.

Tim Kendall

John Allan Wyeth's Dead Landscapes

'I adore war,' Julian Grenfell wrote to his mother in October 1914. 'It's like a big picnic without the objectlessness of a picnic.' Although picnics may be proverbially pleasant, Grenfell detects something frivolous about the picnicker. War is no picnic, but only because it has a purpose, as he goes on to explain: 'The fighting-excitement vitalises everything... One loves one's fellow man so much more when one is bent on killing him.'

Almost the entire war later, on 16 August 1918, First Lieutenant John Allan Wyeth of the US 33rd Division was travelling in a sidecar on the road from Harbonnières to headquarters at Molliens-au-Bois. He had been tasked with delivering maps to an American regiment located somewhere among Australian troops, and after several days of searching, he had arrived too late: the maps—the regiment's colonel wryly informed him—' "might be useful in another war" '. On the way back from his fool's errand, Wyeth passed through the village of Bayonvillers, which lay in ruins after an artillery battle that had ousted the occupying Germans a week earlier. His sonnet describing what he saw, smelled and tasted there is titled 'Picnic':

A house marked 𝕺𝖗𝖙𝖘𝖐𝖔𝖒𝖒𝖆𝖓𝖉𝖆𝖓𝖙𝖚𝖗—a great
sign 𝕶𝖆𝖎𝖘𝖊𝖗𝖕𝖑𝖆𝖙𝖟 on a corner of the church,
and German street names all around the square.
Troop columns split to let our sidecar through.
"Drive like hell and get back on the main road—it's getting late."
"Yessir."

The roadway seemed to reel and lurch
through clay wastes rimmed and pitted everywhere.
"You hungry?—Have some of this, there's enough for two."
We drove through Bayonvillers—and as we ate
men long since dead reached out and left a smirch
and taste in our throats like gas and rotten jam.
"Want any more?"
                    "Yes sir, if you got enough there."
"Those fellows smell pretty strong."
                                        "I'll say they do,
but I'm too hungry sir to care a damn."

'Picnic' was first published in Wyeth's only volume of poetry, *This Man's Army: A War in Fifty-Odd Sonnets* (1928). It demonstrates just how odd those sonnets can be, with a rhyme scheme of Wyeth's own invention (*abcdabcdabecde*) and an extraordinarily acute ear for the pentameter-busting rhythms of everyday conversation as he strings vernacular dialogue across his lines. Wyeth records the difference between ' "Yessir" ' and ' "Yes sir" ', the snatches of abbreviated speech (' "You hungry?", ' "if you got enough there" '), and the balance between a formal acknowledgement of rank and a relaxed familiarity (' "I'm too hungry sir to care a damn" ').

Among his contemporaries, perhaps only Robert Frost matches that nuanced appreciation of the speaking voice. Frost's theory of the 'sound of sense' required that the reader be 'at no loss to give his voice the posture proper to the sentences.' Wyeth's skill in this respect is exemplified by the urgency of his great clumsy line ' "Drive like hell and get back on the main road—it's getting late." ' After the poem's opening description, disturbed by changes in font more than metre, fear becomes suddenly audible as composure slips amidst the cascade of awkward syllables and the ungainly repetition of 'get' and 'getting'.

Why, though, of all titles, 'Picnic'? Is this an example of Grenfellian insouciance and bravado, or of Sassoonish irony? Or could it simply be that a picnic is a picnic is a picnic? After all, food is shared in open air on a kind of excursion—and where better than in France, home of the *pique-nique*? For one startling moment, it even appears possible that this social event will turn into a breaking of bread with the dead, who 'reach... out' as if hungry to participate, only to end up more 'taste[d]' than tasting. 'The rank stench of their bodies haunts me still,' Siegfried Sassoon wrote while out of the line, but this is mood music compared with the gross physicality of Wyeth's 'smirch' in the throat, and his connoisseur's palate as he identifies the flavours of 'gas and rotten jam'. (Few things are more effective than 'rotten jam' when it comes to ruining a picnic.)

Issues of taste—literal and figurative—are the poem's key ingredient, which is why it should have a title that risks seeming tasteless. Wyeth is also cunningly aware that the word 'picnic' can mean different and, for that matter, contradictory things, depending on whose English you happen to be speaking. The phrase 'no picnic' dates from 1888, with *OED* recording its use in Kipling's *Wee Willie Winkie*: ' "Taint no bloomin' picnic in those parts I can tell you." ' It was common enough by 1914 to feature prominently in 'Who's for the Game?', Jessie Pope's notorious recruitment jingle:

> Who knows it won't be a picnic—not much—
> Yet eagerly shoulders a gun?
> Who would much rather come back with a crutch
> Than lie low and be out of the fun?

What complicates matters is that *OED* also records a near-contemporaneous and peculiarly Australasian meaning of 'picnic'—'Used ironically of an awkward situation or a difficult or unpleasant experience'—and gives a first example from E. E. Morris's *Austral English* in 1896: 'If a man's horse is awkward and gives him trouble, he will say, "I had a picnic with that horse", and so of any misadventure or disagreeable experience in travelling.' Not for nothing is 'Picnic' sandwiched, so to speak, between sonnets that incorporate Australian voices. The title stands, bald and brief, as a site and emblem of cultural exchange for French, British English (the word having been introduced into the language by the Earl of Chesterfield), Australian English, and Wyeth's own American English.

This Man's Army is a factually detailed and chronological account of Wyeth's war, from embarcation in May 1918 to his being evacuated out on a hospital train in October of the same year, as victim of an epidemic more deadly than fighting (' "Where was you wounded, Bud?" / "Aw I'm not wounded Buddy—it's just the flu" '). A gifted linguist with a degree in languages from Princeton, Wyeth saw no front-line action but served as a liaison officer between the US army and its allies. Uniquely, the 33rd Division fell under British command for a time, as well as operating alongside Australian forces, so Wyeth found himself translating between English accents and dialects as often as between English and French. ' "Wot-o," ' says an English major by way of greeting, only to be met with a barely comprehensible response: ' "Shake hands with my bunkie—when he ain't cockeyed / he's a damn good egg." ' Small wonder that *This Man's Army* ends with a glossary comprising far more English words than French, crammed as the sonnets are with army slang ('Archies', 'slumgullion', 'monkey-meat') and lines from popular songs that can sound utterly nonsensical out of context (' *Well, I swan, I must / b'gettin on,* (fft) *Giddup, Napoleon it looks like rain*'). And Wyeth is always sharply aware that it does not need as many as two nations to be divided by the same language. As his local French host complains on one occasion, ' "Les Parisiens ne pouvaient rien comprendre / de notre patois." '

After *This Man's Army*, Wyeth made the calamitous decision to give up poetry and dedicate his life to landscape painting, forsaking genius in favour of mere talent. It is surprising, then, that the landscapes of his poetry are dead ground. The sequence opens with Wyeth awaiting sailing orders at Camp Upton: 'Raw barracks blistering in a waste of sand / and scrubby oak and scrawny stunted pine.' It is a 'desolate place, / a desert, even in the month of May.' The French summer delivers no improvement. The 'clay wastes' of Bayonvillers remember that American 'waste of sand'. Elsewhere in France, hillsides are 'leprous' and 'wasted', trees are 'barren' and 'gouty', and in a distant echo of Keats's 'La Belle Dame sans Merci', 'no birds gather in the empty skies'. As a constant reminder of mortality, the poems are coated in dust: a 'dusty square', a 'drifting dust cloud', 'white dust', 'dusty tree trunks', a 'dusty village', 'dusty wreckage', a 'dusty sunset'. War, evidently, can defeat nature; it can even defeat the primeval trope of seasonal renewal, leaving nothing but dust and waste.

Even so, despite the ever-present proximity of death—'How can I sleep with Verdun over there!'—*This Man's Army* refuses to despair. The insistence on dust leads to the predictable allusion, but this occurs at the end of a blues song, not the Anglican Burial Service that might have been expected: '*Ashes to ashes and dust to dust* / […] / *If the* whis*key don't* get *you then the cocaine* must.' We may all be dust, but we go down talking and eating and joking and singing together. Each act of communication—comic or clumsy, misheard or misunderstood though it may be—represents a tiny victory in the eternal battle against war's destructions.

Dead ground is what remains in Wyeth's work when speech is taken away. *This Man's Army* may belong among the most garrulous of poetry collections, but there are two distinct groups who do not participate in the redemptive pleasures of linguistic exchange. Defeated and demoralised in their different ways, they are brought together in the sequence's penultimate sonnet, 'Hospital':

Fever, and crowds—and light that cuts your eyes—
Men waiting in a long slow-shuffling line
with silent private faces, white and bleak.
Long rows of lumpy stretchers on the floor.
My helmet drops—a head jerks up and cries
wide-eyed and settles in a quivering whine.
The air is rank with touching human reek.
A troop of Germans clatters through the door.
They cross our line and something in me dies.
Sullen, detached, obtuse—men into swine—

and hurt unhappy things that walk apart.
Their rancid bodies trail a languid streak
so curious that hate breaks down before
the dull and cruel laughter in my heart.

In 'Picnic' and other poems, speech irrupts to celebrate the persistence of the human spirit. 'Hospital' offers no such reprieve. It is not quite metrically uniform: line 1 starts with a trochee ('Févĕr'), for example, and line 2 with a spondee ('Mén waít | ǐng'). Yet the divergences from iambic pentameter are fewer and further between, as if to suggest that the sonnet's speechless conformity is another kind of dead ground. Appropriately, 'Hospital' opens with a series of static images lacking an active verb, the effect being to drain the scene of energy. The adjectives pile up to form a study in enervation: 'long slow-shuffling line', 'silent private faces, white and bleak', 'long rows', 'lumpy stretchers', 'cries wide-eyed', 'quivering whine', 'Sullen, detached, obtuse', 'hurt unhappy things', 'rancid bodies', 'languid streak', 'so curious', 'dull and cruel laughter'. 'Touching human reek' briefly suggests some kind of human sympathy, but the phrase reanimates the physicality of 'touching' to reverse the word's more usually positive connotations. The 'reek' is so 'rank'—a disgusted repetition of consonants—that it molests the body, like the smirch left by the dead who reach out in 'Picnic'.

Wyeth was fluent in German, and would spend much of the 1930s living and working in Germany as an artist. (The military historian B. J. Omanson has gathered strong circumstantial evidence that he may have been passing on intelligence to the US government.) Even so, the only German words included in *This Man's Army* are 'Ortskommandantur' and 'Kaiserplatz'—both lifted out of the surrounding text and rendered conspicuously alien by their font—and the mildly derogatory term 'Heinie' for the young pilot of an enemy plane that has been shot down. If anyone should be inclined to view the enemy as brothers and mirror-images, it is Wyeth, but here they are unreachably bestial ('men into swine') because they exist outside language. 'Hospital' exudes a visceral loathing, as far from sentimental scenes of football matches in no man's land as it is possible to imagine. With 'rancid', Wyeth finds a word even more nauseating than 'rank' and 'reek'.

The very presence of these Germans is enough to make something in the poet die, and although briefly it seems as though their 'hurt' and their unhappiness might inspire pity, something far more terrible is born. The poet's 'hate breaks down before'—and in the pause created by the line break the reader may expect any number of conciliatory gestures. But to hate someone is, at least, to recognise them as human. Instead of replacing hatred with uplifting recognitions of shared suffering and values, Wyeth describes a response more viciously contemptuous: 'the dull and cruel laughter in my heart'. This is the laughter of the victor over the sullen vanquished, a delighted schadenfreude as the enemy's humanity is stripped away. Never mind the canonical trench lyrics with their tableaux of disfigurement and death: there is no more terrible poem of the War than Wyeth's 'Hospital'.

Although 'Hospital' comes perilously close to the end of *This Man's Army*, and would serve as a bitter signing-off, the antidote to war has been present all along. It is even present in 'Hospital', which makes the case by negative example. War results when there is no bridge between nations and languages and cultures, whereas friendship—which is, rather than peace, the true opposite of war—relies on the kinds of exchange epitomised by the role of the translator. Contrast 'Hospital' with one of Wyeth's wildest and most exuberant sonnets, 'Entente Cordiale':

"You ready, Joe?"
            "Yessir."
                        —"Messieurs, à table!
Ici, mon commandant."
            "That's right, you tell 'em where,
we none of us savvy their lingo."
                        —"Voilà, messieurs."
"Who paint thees card? 'Tis 'ow you say, a *peach*—
de eagle shake 'and weet de coc—C'est admirable!"

"Where's the *soup* Joe—*What?* Which wine first? We don't care,
get 'em tight as quick as you can."
                                    "Ils sont fameux
ces Américains, avec leurs bouteilles!"
                                    "*We*'ll teach
'em to drink."
                    "Mais qu'est-ce que c'est qu'*ça*? C'est *form*i*dable*!"
"My God Joe, you served all four courses at once!"
                                                    "Hey there—
speech, Commaundaunt."
                        "I regrette not to speak."
"Come on there Skipper, it's your turn—Give 'em a speech."
"Bottoms up, men!"
                    "A la santé des deux
républiques!"
                "Yea—*Vive* la *France*!"
                                    "Vive l'*Amérique*!"

Speech in Wyeth's work is a fine excess, spilling over the boundaries of
the pentameter line. Neither his British soldier-poet contemporaries,
nor anyone else in the long history of the sonnet form, ever sounds
remotely like this. Nothing survives of Wyeth's comments on poetry, or
more specifically on his own work, except for a short letter in which a
friend reports his opinions: 'I don't know whether I think he's justified
in calling them sonnets—do you? And he admits that many of these
are not sonnet subjects, but he thought, on the whole, that a modified
sonnet form was the best for the sequence.' Almost the only review of
the volume concluded that the sonnets 'are probably not poetry, but
they are good stuff.' This worrying about labels continues into recent
times, with one commentator arguing that 'this versification is not
what I would call poetry… [It] is not art, not even street (or trench)
art. It's a mere curiosity.'

So much the worse for the sonnet and for poetry if 'Entente
Cordiale' fails to qualify simply because it plays havoc with convention.

Macaronic, interlingual—these terms cannot do justice to the vivacious experimentalism of a work that veers giddily from English to Franglais to French and back again. The glorious irony in that admission ' "We none of us savvy their lingo" '—'savvy' from the French *savoir* and 'lingo' sharing a root with 'langue'—alerts the reader (or, rather, listener) to Wyeth's extensive use of linguistic parallels: table/table, paint/peindre, commandant/commandant, peach/pêche, admirable/admirable, card/carte, turn/tour, serve/servir, soup/soupe, eagle/aigle, cockerel/coq, bottles/bouteilles, famous/fameux, formidable/formidable, wine/vin, regret/regrette, republic/république, France/France, America/Amérique, and the poem's title and conclusion that need no translation. 'Entente Cordiale' is a brilliant comic performance. If war and nature are dead ground, the living ground is that ever-shifting polyglot melange in which Wyeth's sonnet sequence is billeted.

Don McCullin, 'The Battlefields of the Somme, France, 2000'

Jeremy Mynott

Nature's Ground

'Landscapes have more ways of surviving death
than people do.'

THERE IS A classic description by 'Saki' (H. H. Munro) of the effects of
trench warfare on the birdlife of the western front in the First World
War. The owls did very well, he tells us, especially the barn owls, which
had an ample supply of food in the rats and mice that infested the
fighting lines and plenty of ruined buildings in which to nest. Similarly,
kestrels and sparrowhawks thrived (though apparently not buzzards,
perhaps because they depended on larger mammals for their prey?).
Partridges and skylarks continued to rear their broods in land 'seamed
and bisected with trenches and honeycombed with shell-holes'. Even
the shy members of the crow family held their ground:

> The rook is normally so gun-shy and nervous where noise
> is concerned that the sharp banging of a barn-door or the
> report of a toy pistol will sometimes set an entire rookery
> in commotion; out here I have seen him sedately busy
> among the refuse heaps of a battered village, with shells
> bursting at no great distance, and the impatient-sounding
> snapping rattle of machine-guns going on all round him;
> for all the notice that he took he might have been in some
> peaceful English meadow on a sleepy Sunday afternoon.
> Whatever else German frightfulness may have done it has
> not frightened the rook of northern France; it has made
> his nerves steadier than they have ever been before, and

future generations of small boys, employed in scaring rooks away from the sown crops in this region, will have to invent something in the way of super-frightfulness to achieve their purpose.

In the case of magpies, there was a reversal of the usual roles. They had been driven from many of their traditional nesting sites, but they had become bolder than their human persecutors in the 'no man's land' between the trenches:

> Affection for a particular tree has in one case induced a pair of magpies to build their bulky domed nest in the battered remains of a poplar of which so little remained standing that the nest looked almost bigger than the tree; the effect rather suggested an arch-episcopal enthronement taking place in the ruined remains of Melrose Abbey. The magpie, wary and suspicious in his wild state, must be rather intrigued at the change that has come over his erstwhile fearsome not-to-be-avoided human, stalking everywhere over the earth as its possessor, who now creeps about in screened and sheltered ways, as chary of showing himself in the open as the shyest of wild creatures.

And some 2,300 years earlier, Thucydides had described how the scavengers that followed great warring armies actually benefitted from the human carnage. Dogs, eagles and vultures glutted themselves on the corpses and only desisted when the cause of death was not human violence but the devastating (and still unidentified) plague that swept through Athens in 430–429BC:

> Despite there being many unburied bodies the birds and animals which feed on human flesh either kept away from the corpses or if they started eating them died themselves. The evidence for this is that there was a marked absence of such birds, which were not to be seen around the bodies or anywhere else at all.

War zones of the kind Saki described, even though they involve serious damage to the landscape, soon recover anyway. The blood-red poppy of the Flanders fields led and symbolized such a regeneration.

Other violent changes are more natural—that is, if extreme weather events still count as natural. The Great Storm of 1987 in Britain was such an event. On 15–16 October of that year hurricane-force winds overnight changed many familiar landscapes in southern England in what was literally the most radical way, uprooting and flattening some fifteen million trees. It produced not just physical chaos but also emotional trauma, and it changed some long-held beliefs about how to manage the environment. The head forester of the National Trust described it as follows:

> The initial response to the storm was urgent. It was an instinct. Something awful had happened to places people loved. They were devastated and it had to be put right immediately. After a while, we stopped to ask why it matters, why are trees and woodlands so important? It became about human need … and we explored ways of working with nature.

There were significant effects on birdlife, of course, but not all negative. Fallen trees were left to regenerate, new plantings were undertaken, glades and open spaces emerged, some heathland reappeared, tribes of insects thrived on the fallen timber, birds thrived on the insects, and woodlarks, tree pipits, and nightjars re-colonised areas from which they had long departed. In short, the wildlife changed and adapted. This was the largest storm of its kind in Britain since 1703, though we are told they may now become more frequent. In other parts of the world they are already common, indeed so regular as to be part of the seasonal experience. What was especially upsetting in England was the speed and scale of the disruption. We were grieving not only the loss of familiar landscapes but also the loss of our familiar responses to it.

Other kinds of landscape change can be engineered more deliberately and have longer-lasting effects. The classic example here was the Enclosure Movement of the eighteenth and nineteenth centuries, whereby common land was by Act of Parliament 'enclosed' and parcelled out into private lots. John Clare was the authentic voice of protest. He found the reconfiguration of the countryside he knew so intimately to be profoundly alienating, and in poems such as 'The Lamentation of Round-Oak Waters' and 'The Lament of Swordy Well', he imagines the land itself speaking out against its abuse:

> Of all the fields I am the last
> That my own face can tell.
> Yet, what with stone pits' delving holes
> And strife to buy and sell,
> My name will quickly be the whole
> That's left of Swordy Well.

Indeed, in 'The Moors' he counts the birds themselves as much the victims of the new laws of trespass as were the poor:

> Each little tyrant with his little sign
> Shows where man claims, earth glows no more divine.
> On paths to freedom and to childhood dear
> A board sticks up to notice "no road here"
> And on the tree with ivy overhung
> The hated sign by vulgar taste is hung
> As though the very birds should learn to know
> When they go there they must no further go.
> Thus, with the poor, scared freedom bade goodbye
> And much they feel it in the smothered sigh,
> And birds and trees and flowers without a name
> All sighed when lawless law's enclosure came . . .

Clare was responding to changes less violent and sudden than those arising from war or hurricane but in some ways more insidious, far-reaching and long-lasting. These were changes we had willed, as part of a deliberate political process. Clare had lost his bearings and was, as he said 'out of his knowledge' in this changed landscape. One particularly poignant personal consequence was that he had himself to seek employment in planting and establishing the detested new hedgerows.

There was also a larger historical and cultural irony, of course, since one effect of the changes he deplored was the landscape of small fields and hedgerows that we in turn have found attractive and have sought to defend against subsequent changes to agricultural practice. Birds form part of the rhetoric of defence, for us as well as for Clare. There is one real difference, however. In both cases the birds react and adapt, with consequent changes in distribution and populations; but in our day, largely as a consequence of intensive agriculture, the adaptation has taken the form not just of change, as some species replace others, but of disappearance and retreat, with a clear overall impoverishment and loss of diversity.

In the last fifty years or so Britain has lost over half its wildlife, including over 60% of our skylarks, lapwing and cuckoos, and a staggering 90% or more of our grey partridges and turtle doves. These and many other much-loved species are deeply embedded in our cultural history, familiar reference points whose absence in the 'silent spring' of modern arable farmlands will eventually empty the countryside of its metaphorical as well as its living significance. This too is a kind of 'dead ground'.

Clare's social sympathies were with the displaced poor, but his reaction also sounds like an extreme case of conservatism, arising from his intimate affinity with the land and his deep identification with it. So far from sentimentalising the land through the poetic device of a personification into which he projects his own feelings, Clare may be doing exactly the reverse, echoing the sorrows of the land of which he felt himself an indigenous part. Was he perhaps anticipating the sort of ecological ideas associated with the Gaia hypothesis of James Lovelock, the idea that the whole earth is a single, living ecosystem with its own interests and reactions? That notion was initially dismissed as anthropomorphic fantasy, but it may come to seem more attractive as science increasingly records the diffusion of 'intelligence' throughout an ever-widening circle of animate life, including not only mammals and birds but also a wide range of invertebrates like octopus and social insects and even plants.

Clare was a poet, however, not a theorist. What these and the earlier quotations illustrate is the thought—which goes beyond the province of science alone—that the idea of 'nature' is by no means a simple one and that there are no easy distinctions between natural and human landscapes or between wild and artificial ones.

But did the Great Storm replace one natural landscape with another one, or were both equally manmade? Was the Storm itself natural? Were Clare's wild moors not themselves an unnatural effect of an earlier deforestation? Is a hedge more natural than an open field? The ravaged battle-fields of World War I were arenas of creation as well as destruction, at least for the wildlife for whom our wars were incidental to their purposes.

There are of course real differences between the human and the nonhuman world, but as the critic Raymond Williams once famously observed, 'The idea of nature contains, though often unnoticed, an extraordinary amount of human history.' Even the idea of landscape is an artificial one: a 'land-scape' is literally land as painted or seen by a human viewer, and the word itself was invented only in the seventeenth century, first to denote a kind of painting and then later the scenery represented in it.

One can at best think of 'the natural' as a kind of continuum, though one with many discontinuities and dimensions. At one end might be totally artificial constructions like Wild Blue Yokohama in Japan, which is a massive indoor beach with simulated waves, palm trees, sand, rivers, and rain forest—a manufactured paradise interspersed with convenient sunlamps and Jacuzzis and without the discomforts of scorpions, jellyfish or bad weather. In this confection of concrete and rubber, refugees from the city can safely explore 'the great indoors'.

At the other end might be the Antarctic continent, still populated by only about one thousand people in the winter months in its 5.4 million square miles, but of course wholly dependent for its wildness on human decisions to keep it so, and in that sense also an artificial construct and one vulnerable in any case to climate change, which itself has human origins to some degree. In between these extremes are the majority of the world's habitats and environments, none of them untouched by change or by human history.

Landscapes have more ways of surviving death than people do. Even the exclusion zone at Chernobyl is being repopulated by animals like bear, wolves and deer moving back into territory judged too dangerous for human occupation, though what long-term genetic damage they may suffer from persisting radiation levels there is as yet unknown. The natural world may not be infinitely adaptable, however, unless you define it just as whatever survives even after metamorphic change of the kind threatened by nuclear holocaust or another mass extinction in the new geological era now dubbed the Anthropocene. But that would be an empty definition, in every sense. 'Dead ground' in [WWI] military parlance literally meant the terrain between opposing forces that was hidden to observers. I have been exploring more metaphorical extensions of the term, though in these extreme apocalyptic scenarios where the observers themselves are eliminated we move beyond the reach even of metaphor.

Andrew Motion

The Hawthorn

In memory of Private James Crozier
executed in Picardie, 27 February 1916

There is no question of day breaking
suddenly—one minute slow darkness
the next sunlight like a blind drawn up.
There is seepage. A thing not happening
then over and done with in a twinkling.
Although what is revealed stays the same:
a tilting three acre field of rough grazing;
the brown boot-stamp of last winter's rain
refusing to fade from the steepest angle;
clumps of loose-knit but tangled clover;
a skyline of trees like exclamation marks;
and staggering at dead centre a hawthorn
managing to hold its ground but barely.

*

This hawthorn has been cringing forward
like a seriously shy child who never meant
to be the subject of this or any photograph.
A child who in the space of a few yards grew
into an adult and lost control—wild hair,
flapping rags of a trench coat, soft muttering

*How did I get here, who am I, why am I here
alone*, but still beautiful as battalions of cloud
parade overhead in their dull grey uniforms,
keeping the allowance of light to a minimum
which is enough nevertheless to show sharp
spikes of frost prickling the hawthorn's hands
clasped to its face even when a breeze arrives
and seeks to remove them, fails, and sweeps on.

*

Except no one can ever find this beautiful now,
things being as they are, not that the hawthorn
would yet have stepped on its delicate tiptoe
away from the hedgerow and down the brown
slope of wintry grass towards the clover patch
when dawn broke on the 27th February 1916,
not that its icy spikes and stiff gesticulations
would have appeared to Private James Crozier
as the last evidence of Picardie and the world,
the hawthorn and beauty impossible to consider
would only have come to pass in the aftermath,
when parent trees on the skyline took a chance
and ushered or let creep forward one of their own
to stall and dither and dishevel out in the open,
to fall and die here in due course still unregarded.

Acknowledgements

FIRST THE EDITORS want to thank the contributors for their marvellous response to the project and for meeting their deadlines, revised or unrevised, in good time to keep this book on track for its crucial November publication date. They have together made an inspirational publication and we are deeply grateful to them.

For permission to quote in full Henry Reed's 'Judging Distances' we thank Eileen Gunn and the Royal Literary Fund.

The images of Nelson's Pillar in Dublin have been provided by the National Library of Ireland (Irish Political Scenes Collection and Michael S. Walker Collection) and we acknowledge our indebtedness to the NLI and its permissions staff. We thank Ian Ritchie and Ian Ritchie Architects for permitting us to use the two images of 'The Spire'. The image with Larkin's statue is © Ian Ritchie Architects, photograph by Barry Mason.

We are grateful to Tate Images, Tate Gallery, and Don McCullin for permission to reprint 'The Battlefields of the Somme, France'; and similarly thank Tate Images for allowing us to print the image of Paul Nash's 'Totes Meer' (1941). The Imperial War Museum has kindly granted permission for use of images of the following paintings by Paul Nash: 'The Ypres Salient at Night', 1918; 'We Are Making a New World', 1918; 'The Menin Road', 1919; 'The Battle of Britain', 1941; 'The Battle of Germany', 1944. We are especially grateful to Sebastian Wainwright of the IWM.

Brian Turner has generously allowed us to reprint 'Smoking with the Dead and Wounded', which first appeared in the *Georgia Review* (Fall, 2015).

Carcanet Press have given permission to reprint 'In Memory of Private Roberts' from *Nevermore* (2000) by Andrew McNeillie.

We are grateful to Neil Astley and Suzanne Fairless-Aitken of Bloodaxe for permission to quote extensively from the work of Isabel Palmer ('Atmospherics', in the volume *Home Front* (2016)) and from Brian Turner's *Here, Bullet* (2007) both in Kate McLoughlin's essay.

T. R. Henn's poem on 'To Wilton House' is reproduced in full by kind permission of Colin Smythe and the Estate of T. R. Henn.

For his expertise and great patience in designing the book and type-setting the text we wish to thank Michael Johnson of Oxgarth Design. And for special help regarding the cover we thank: Paul Hodgson for the overall design, and Tom Garside and Gail McNeillie for their images.

*   *   *

Damian Walford Davies wishes to thank Elizabeth Ennion-Smith, archivist at St Catherine's College, Cambridge, for supporting his researches.

Tim Kendall notes his indebtedness to B. J. Omanson, who redis-covered *This Man's Army* and helped to bring it back into print. The 2008 edition, published by the University of South Carolina Press, contains extensive annotations by Omanson detailing the movements of the 33rd Division and Wyeth's role within it.

James Macdonald Lockhart acknowledges the work and assistance of Fraser MacDonald from the Institute of Geography, University of Edinburgh, in particular his essays, 'Doomsday Fieldwork, or, How to Rescue Gaelic Culture?' (*Environment and Planning D: Society and Space* 2011, vol. 29, 309–335); 'The Last Outpost of Empire: Rockall and the Cold War' (*Journal of Historical Geography*, 32 (2006) 627–647) and 'Geopolitics and "the vision thing": regarding Britain and America's first nuclear missile' (*Transactions of the Institute of British Geographers*, 31, 53–71, 2006). The section on 'nuclear language' draws on a paper by Carol Cohn titled 'Slick' Ems, Glick' Ems, Christmas Trees, and Cookie Cutters: Nuclear Language and how we Learned to Pat the Bomb' (*Bulletin of the Atomic Scientists*, June 1987, vol. 43, no. 5, 17–25).

To learn more about the murals of Northern Ireland, google: Tony Crowley mni; or visit http://ccdl.libraries.claremont.edu/cdm/landing page/collection/mni

Index

This is not an exhaustive index but one of selected names (excluding contributors), concepts and phenomena that readers might find interesting to follow up.

Binyon, Laurence: 'Bin-Bin' and Ezra
Pound, 185
Blair, Tony: and Sykes-Picot, xv
Blake, William: and Paul Nash, 172
Blunden, Edmund: household name,
xviii; Graves distrusted by, 186; and
Marsh and Georgianism, Graves's
'sacred charge', poems lost in mud,
predominantly a pastoralist, and
Collins and Clare, 188; *works*:
Undertones of War, 186, 188; 'Third
Ypres', 188–9
Bobrowski, Johannes: German poet,
and the Scottish war poets, 154
Bomberg, David: painter, of famous
generation, and Paul Nash, 172
Borden, Mary: 'the extraordinary', 187
Bottomley, Gordon: Georgian poet's
mark not made, 189
British Army: Parachute Regiment in
Helmand, 2–6; blunders and crises,
4; dashing Pathfinder Platoon,
6; Royal Logistical Corps, 7; and
kinetic euphemism, 8; its soldiers
'believe in happy endings', 11;
Royal Gurkha Rifles, and Black
Watch, 12; Queen's Own Gurkha
Logistics Regiment, 13; the nature
of soldiering, 17, and of being a
soldier, 18, 19, 20; Rifles Regiment,
father and son, 41; commando
training, and SAS selection
casualties, 43; training for war,
FIBUA skills and FISH & CHIPS,
78; on Mynydd Epynt, 80, 'beyond
East Germany', and the Burma
Road, … a 'colonising continuum',
and at Tyneham, 81; Otterburn
ranges, and *Sci-fi Lullabies* by
Suede, 83; bird-watching in the
Hebrides, and Danger Areas,
88, 89, 90, 92; and NATO, 92;
in the north of Ireland,108, 109,

110, 117–24; and the Irish border,
118–19; paratroopers, and Scots
regiments in childhood Ireland,
123; almost nothing left behind,
123–4; and Southern Command,
at Wilton House, 127–8; Philip
Larkin unfit for, 137; and George
Campbell Hay, 150; Royal
Ordnance Corp, 152; and notorious
recruitment jingle, 'Who's for the
Game?', 193; Private James Crozier,
executed, 209; *see also* RAF and
Royal Marines
Brittain, Vera: excluded by Marsh, but
included in *Scars Upon My Heart*,
187
Brooke, Rupert: deluded household
name, xviii; Georgian Poetry, and
his debut collection, 183; sales
rocketed upon his death, 184;
'Rupert Brooke fund', 187; *works*:
'Peace', xvii, 216; 'The Soldier', 184
Buchan, John: his character Sandy
Arbuthnot, and Arabists in
clubland, 34; *see also* Oman
Bugan, Carmen: poet of Romania,
58; brings Ceauşescu to book, 59;
her father Ion, 59, 66–7; 'poems
after surveillance', 60; 'Found in
secret police records', 60; Fellow of
the Orwell Prize, 60; 'Childhood
under the Eye of the Secret
Police', 63; found in translation,
63, dead ground and new terrain,
64; thanks the State Archives,
64; and 'a reticent source', 66;
the Bugan home, bugged, 67–8;
works: *Burying the Typewriter*, 58–9;
Releasing the Porcelain Birds, 59, 63;
'A birthday letter', 65; 'There', 66
Bukharin, Nicolai *see* Mandelstam,
Osip